THE ART OF CONTROVERSY

THE ART OF CONTROVERSY

And Other Posthumous Papers

BY

ARTHUR SCHOPENHAUER

Si quis, toto die currens, pervenit ad vesperam, satis est
PETRARCH : *DE VERA SAPIENTIA*

SELECTED AND TRANSLATED

BY

T. BAILEY SAUNDERS, M.A.

LONDON : GEORGE ALLEN & UNWIN LTD.
RUSKIN HOUSE   40 MUSEUM STREET, W.C.

First Published 1896
Reprinted. . 1921

THE ABERDEEN UNIVERSITY PRESS LIMITED.

TRANSLATOR'S PREFACE.

THE volume now before the reader is a tardy addition to a series in which I have endeavoured to present Schopenhauer's minor writings in an adequate form.

Its contents are drawn entirely from his posthumous papers. A selection of them was given to the world some three or four years after his death by his friend and literary executor, Julius Frauenstädt, who, for this and other offices of piety, has received less recognition than he deserves. The papers then published have recently been issued afresh, with considerable additions and corrections, by Dr. Eduard Grisebach, who is also entitled to gratitude for the care with which he has followed the text of the manuscripts, now in the Royal Library at Berlin, and for having drawn attention—although in terms that are unnecessarily severe—to a number of faults and failings on the part of the previous editor.

The fact that all Schopenhauer's works, together with a volume of his correspondence, may now be obtained in a certain cheap collection of the best national and foreign literature displayed in almost every bookshop in Germany, is sufficient evidence that in his own country the writer's popularity is still very great; nor does the demand for translations indicate that his fame has at all diminished abroad. The

favour with which the new edition of his posthumous papers has been received induces me, therefore, to resume a task which I thought, five years ago,
that I had finally completed; and it is my intention
to bring out one more volume, selected partly from
these papers and partly from his *Parerga.*

A small part of the essay on *The Art of Controversy*
was published in Schopenhauer's lifetime, in the
chapter of the *Parerga* headed *Zur Logik und
Dialektik.* The intelligent reader will discover that
a good deal of its contents is of an ironical character.
As regards the last three essays I must observe
that I have omitted such passages as appear to be no
longer of any general interest or otherwise unsuitable.
I must also confess to having taken one or two
liberties with the titles, in order that they may the
more effectively fulfil the purpose for which titles
exist. In other respects I have adhered to the
original with the kind of fidelity which aims at pro-
ducing an impression as nearly as possible similar to
that produced by the original.

T. B. S.

February, 1896.

CONTENTS.

	PAGE
THE ART OF CONTROVERSY—	
1. PRELIMINARY: LOGIC AND DIALECTIC	1
2. THE BASIS OF ALL DIALECTIC	13
3. STRATAGEMS	15
ON THE COMPARATIVE PLACE OF INTEREST AND BEAUTY IN WORKS OF ART	49
PSYCHOLOGICAL OBSERVATIONS	63
ON THE WISDOM OF LIFE: APHORISMS	75
GENIUS AND VIRTUE	99

THE ART OF CONTROVERSY.

PRELIMINARY: LOGIC AND DIALECTIC.

By the ancients, Logic and Dialectic were used as synonymous terms; although λογίζεσθαι, "to think over, to consider, to calculate," and διαλέγεσθαι, "to converse," are two very different things.

The name Dialectic was, as we are informed by Diogenes Laertius, first used by Plato; and in the *Phædrus*, *Sophist*, *Republic*, bk. vii., and elsewhere, we find that by Dialectic he means the regular employment of the reason, and skill in the practice of it. Aristotle also uses the word in this sense; but, according to Laurentius Valla, he was the first to use Logic too in a similar way.[1] Dialectic, therefore, seems to be an older word than Logic. Cicero and Quintilian use the words in the same general signification.[2]

---

[1] He speaks of δυσχερείαι λογικαλ, that is, "difficult points," πρότασις λογικὴ, ἀπορία λογικὴ.

[2] Cic. *in Lucullo: Dialecticam inventam esse, veri et falsi quasi disceptatricem.* Topica, c. 2: *Stoici enim judicandi vias diligenter persecuti sunt, ea scientia, quam* Dialecticen *appellant.* Quint., lib. ii., 12: *Itaque hæc pars dialecticae, sive illam disputatricem dicere malimus;* and with him this latter word appears to be the Latin equivalent for Dialectic. (So far according to "Petri Rami dialectica, Audomari Talaei praelectionibus illustrata". 1569.)

This use of the words as synonymous terms lasted
through the Middle Ages into modern times; in fact,
until the present day.   But more recently, and in
particular by Kant, Dialectic has often been employed
in a bad sense, as meaning "the art of sophistical controversy"; and hence Logic has been preferred, as of
the two the more innocent designation.   Nevertheless, both originally meant the same thing; and in the
last few years they have again been recognised as
synonymous.

It is a pity that the words have thus been used
from of old, and that I am not quite at liberty to
distinguish their meanings.   Otherwise, I should have
preferred to define *Logic* (from λόγος, "word" and
"reason," which are inseparable) as "the science of the
laws of thought, that is, of the method of reason";
and *Dialectic* (from διαλέγεσθαι, "to converse"—and
every conversation communicates either facts or
opinions, that is to say, it is historical or deliberative)
as "the art of disputation," in the modern sense of the
word.   It is clear, then, that Logic deals with a subject of a purely *à priori* character, separable in
definition from experience, namely, the laws of
thought, the process of reason or the λόγος; the laws,
that is, which reason follows when it is left to itself
and not hindered, as in the case of solitary thought
on the part of a rational being who is in no way
misled.   Dialectic, on the other hand, would treat of
the intercourse between two rational beings who,
because they are rational, ought to think in common,
but who, as soon as they cease to agree like two clocks
keeping exactly the same time, create a disputation,

or intellectual contest. Regarded as purely rational beings, the individuals would, I say, necessarily be in agreement, and their variation springs from the difference essential to individuality; in other words, it is drawn from experience.

Logic, therefore, as the science of thought, or the science of the process of pure reason, should be capable of being constructed à priori. Dialectic, for the most part, can be constructed only à posteriori; that is to say, we may learn its rules by an experiential knowledge of the disturbance which pure thought suffers through the difference of individuality manifested in the intercourse between two rational beings, and also by acquaintance with the means which disputants adopt in order to make good against one another their own individual thought, and to show that it is pure and objective. For human nature is such that if A. and B. are engaged in thinking in common, and are communicating their opinions to one another on any subject, so long as it is not a mere fact of history, and A. perceives that B.'s thoughts on one and the same subject are not the same as his own, he does not begin by revising his own process of thinking, so as to discover any mistake which he may have made, but he assumes that the mistake has occurred in B.'s. In other words, man is naturally obstinate; and this quality in him is attended with certain results, treated of in the branch of knowledge which I should like to call Dialectic, but which, in order to avoid misunderstanding, I shall call Controversial or Eristical Dialectic. Accordingly, it is the branch of knowledge which treats of the obstinacy natural to man. Eristic is only a harsher name for the same thing.

Controversial Dialectic is the art of disputing, and of disputing in such a way as to hold one's own, whether one is in the right or the wrong—*per fas et nefas*.[1] A man may be objectively in the right, and nevertheless in the eyes of bystanders, and sometimes in his own, he may come off worst. For example, I may advance a proof of some assertion, and my adversary may refute the proof, and thus appear to have refuted the assertion, for which there may, nevertheless, be other proofs. In this case, of course,

---

[1] According to Diogenes Laertius, v., 28, Aristotle put Rhetoric and Dialectic together, as aiming at persuasion, $\tau\grave{o}$ $\pi\iota\theta\alpha\nu\acute{o}\nu$; and Analytic and Philosophy as aiming at truth. Aristotle does, indeed, distinguish between (1) *Logic*, or Analytic, as the theory or method of arriving at true or apodeictic conclusions; and (2) *Dialectic* as the method of arriving at conclusions that are accepted or pass current as true, $\acute{\epsilon}\nu\delta o\xi\alpha$, *probabilia*; conclusions in regard to which it is not taken for granted that they are false, and also not taken for granted that they are true in themselves, since that is not the point. What is this but the art of being in the right, whether one has any reason for being so or not, in other words, the art of attaining the appearance of truth, regardless of its substance? That is, then, as I put it above.

Aristotle divides all conclusions into logical and dialectical, in the manner described, and then into eristical. (3) *Eristic* is the method by which the form of the conclusion is correct, but the premisses, the materials from which it is drawn, are not true, but only appear to be true. Finally (4) *Sophistic* is the method in which the form of the conclusion is false, although it seems correct. These three last properly belong to the art of Controversial Dialectic, as they have no objective truth in view, but only the appearance of it, and pay no regard to truth itself; that is to say, they aim at victory. Aristotle's book on *Sophistic Conclusions* was edited apart from the others, and at a later date. It was the last book of his *Dialectic*.

my adversary and I change places: he comes off best, although, as a matter of fact, he is in the wrong.

If the reader asks how this is, I reply that it is simply the natural baseness of human nature. If human nature were not base, but thoroughly honourable, we should in every debate have no other aim than the discovery of truth; we should not in the least care whether the truth proved to be in favour of the opinion which we had begun by expressing, or of the opinion of our adversary. That we should regard as a matter of no moment, or, at any rate, of very secondary consequence; but, as things are, it is the main concern. Our innate vanity, which is particularly sensitive in reference to our intellectual powers, will not suffer us to allow that our first position was wrong and our adversary's right. The way out of this difficulty would be simply to take the trouble always to form a correct judgment. For this a man would have to think before he spoke. But, with most men, innate vanity is accompanied by loquacity and innate dishonesty. They speak before they think; and even though they may afterwards perceive that they are wrong, and that what they assert is false, they want it to seem the contrary. The interest in truth, which may be presumed to have been their only motive when they stated the proposition alleged to be true, now gives way to the interests of vanity: and so, for the sake of vanity, what is true must seem false, and what is false must seem true.

However, this very dishonesty, this persistence in a proposition which seems false even to ourselves, has something to be said for it. It often happens that we begin with the firm conviction of the truth of our statement; but our opponent's argument appears to refute it. Should we abandon our position at once, we may discover later on that we were right after all; the proof we offered was false, but nevertheless there was a proof for our statement which was true. The argument which would have been our salvation did not occur to us at the moment. Hence we make it a rule to attack a counter-argument, even though to all appearances it is true and forcible, in the belief that its truth is only superficial, and that in the course of the dispute another argument will occur to us by which we may upset it, or succeed in confirming the truth of our statement. In this way we are almost compelled to become dishonest; or, at any rate, the temptation to do so is very great. Thus it is that the weakness of our intellect and the perversity of our will lend each other mutual support; and that, generally, a disputant fights not for truth, but for his proposition, as though it were a battle *pro aris et focis*. He sets to work *per fas et nefas*; nay, as we have seen, he cannot easily do otherwise. As a rule, then, every man will insist on maintaining whatever he has said, even though for the moment he may consider it false or doubtful.[1]

[1] Machiavelli recommends his Prince to make use of every moment that his neighbour is weak, in order to attack him; as otherwise his neighbour may do the same. If honour and fidelity prevailed in the world, it would be a different matter; but as these are qualities not to be expected, a man must not practise them himself, because he will meet with a bad return. It is just the same in a dispute: if I allow that my opponent is right as soon as

To some extent every man is armed against such a procedure by his own cunning and villainy. He learns by daily experience, and thus comes to have his own *natural Dialectic*, just as he has his own *natural Logic*. But his Dialectic is by no means as safe a guide as his Logic. It is not so easy for any one to think or draw an inference contrary to the laws of Logic; false judgments are frequent, false conclusions very rare. A man cannot easily be deficient in natural Logic, but he may very easily be deficient in natural Dialectic, which is a gift apportioned in unequal measure. In so far natural Dialectic resembles the faculty of judgment, which differs in degree with every man; while reason, strictly speaking, is the same. For it often happens that in a matter in which a man is really in the right, he is confounded or refuted by merely superficial arguments; and if he emerges victorious from a contest, he owes it very often not so much to the correctness of his judgment in stating his proposition, as to the cunning and address with which he defended it.

Here, as in all other cases, the best gifts are born with a man; nevertheless, much may be done to make

he seems to be so, it is scarcely probable that he will do the same when the position is reversed; and as he acts wrongly, I am compelled to act wrongly too. It is easy to say that we must yield to truth, without any prepossession in favour of our own statements; but we cannot assume that our opponent will do it, and therefore we cannot do it either. Nay, if I were to abandon the position on which I had previously bestowed much thought, as soon as it appeared that he was right, it might easily happen that I might be misled by a momentary impression, and give up the truth in order to accept an error.

him a master of this art by practice, and also by a
consideration of the tactics which may be used to
defeat an opponent, or which he uses himself for a
similar purpose. Therefore, even though Logic may
be of no very real, practical use, Dialectic may certainly be so; and Aristotle, too, seems to me to have
drawn up his Logic proper, or Analytic, as a foundation and preparation for his Dialectic, and to have
made this his chief business. Logic is concerned
with the mere form of propositions: Dialectic, with
their contents or matter—in a word, with their substance. It was proper, therefore, to consider the
general form of all propositions before proceeding to
particulars.

Aristotle does not define the object of Dialectic as
exactly as I have done it here; for while he allows
that its principal object is disputation, he declares
at the same time that it is also the discovery of
truth.[1] Again, he says, later on, that if, from the
philosophical point of view, propositions are dealt
with according to their truth, Dialectic regards them
according to their plausibility, or the measure in
which they will win the approval and assent of
others.[2] He is aware that the objective truth of a
proposition must be distinguished and separated from
the way in which it is pressed home, and approbation
won for it; but he fails to draw a sufficiently sharp
distinction between these two aspects of the matter,
so as to reserve Dialectic for the latter alone.[3] The

---

[1] *Topica*, bk. i., 2.   [2] *Ib.*, 12.

[3] On the other hand, in his book *De Sophisticis Elenchis*, he takes
too much trouble to separate *Dialectic* from *Sophistic* and *Eristic*,

rules which he often gives for Dialectic contain some
of those which properly belong to Logic; and hence

where the distinction is said to consist in this, that dialectical
conclusions are true in their form and their contents, while
sophistical and eristical conclusions are false.

Eristic so far differs from Sophistic that, while the master of
Eristic aims at mere victory, the Sophist looks to the reputation,
and with it, the monetary rewards which he will gain. But
whether a proposition is true in respect of its contents is far too
uncertain a matter to form the foundation of the distinction in
question; and it is a matter on which the disputant least of all
can arrive at certainty; nor is it disclosed in any very sure form
even by the result of the disputation. Therefore, when Aristotle
speaks of *Dialectic*, we must include in it Sophistic, Eristic, and
Peirastic, and define it as " the art of getting the best of it in a
dispute," in which, unquestionably, the safest plan is to be in
the right to begin with; but this in itself is not enough in the
existing disposition of mankind, and, on the other hand, with the
weakness of the human intellect, it is not altogether necessary.
Other expedients are required, which, just because they are unnecessary to the attainment of objective truth, may also be used
when a man is objectively in the wrong; and whether or not this
is the case, is hardly ever a matter of complete certainty.

I am of opinion, therefore, that a sharper distinction should be
drawn between Dialectic and Logic than Aristotle has given us;
that to Logic we should assign objective truth as far as it is merely
formal, and that Dialectic should be confined to the art of gaining
one's point, and contrarily, that Sophistic and Eristic should not
be distinguished from Dialectic in Aristotle's fashion, since the
difference which he draws rests on objective and material truth;
and in regard to what this is, we cannot attain any clear certainty
before discussion; but we are compelled, with Pilate, to ask, *What
is truth?* For truth is in the depths, ἐν βύθῳ ἡ ἀλήθεια (a saying of
Democritus, *Diog. Laert.*, ix., 72). Two men often engage in a warm
dispute, and then return to their homes each of the other's
opinion, which he has exchanged for his own. It is easy to say
that in every dispute we should have no other aim than the advancement of truth; but before dispute no one knows where it is,
and through his opponent's arguments and his own a man is misled.

it appears to me that he has not provided a clear solution of the problem.

We must always keep the subject of one branch of knowledge quite distinct from that of any other. To form a clear idea of the province of Dialectic, we must pay no attention to objective truth, which is an affair of Logic ; we must regard it simply as *the art of getting the best of it in a dispute*, which, as we have seen, is all the easier if we are actually in the right. In itself Dialectic has nothing to do but to show how a man may defend himself against attacks of every kind, and especially against dishonest attacks ; and, in the same fashion, how he may attack another man's statement without contradicting himself, or generally without being defeated. The discovery of objective truth must be separated from the art of winning acceptance for propositions ; for objective truth is an entirely different matter : it is the business of sound judgment, reflection and experience, for which there is no special art.

Such, then, is the aim of Dialectic. It has been defined as the Logic of appearance ; but the definition is a wrong one, as in that case it could only be used to repel false propositions. But even when a man has the right on his side, he needs Dialectic in order to defend and maintain it ; he must know what the dishonest tricks are, in order to meet them ; nay, he must often make use of them himself, so as to beat the enemy with his own weapons.

Accordingly, in a dialectical contest we must put objective truth aside, or, rather, we must regard it as an accidental circumstance, and look only to the defence of our own position and the refutation of our opponent's.

In following out the rules to this end, no respect should be paid to objective truth, because we usually do not know where the truth lies. As I have said, a man often does not himself know whether he is in the right or not ; he often believes it, and is mistaken : both sides often believe it. Truth is in the depths. At the beginning of a contest each man believes, as a rule, that right is on his side ; in the course of it, both become doubtful, and the truth is not determined or confirmed until the close.

Dialectic, then, need have nothing to do with truth, as little as the fencing master considers who is in the right when a dispute leads to a duel. Thrust and parry is the whole business. Dialectic is the art of intellectual fencing ; and it is only when we so regard it that we can erect it into a branch of knowledge. For if we take purely objective truth as our aim, we are reduced to mere Logic ; if we take the maintenance of false propositions, it is mere Sophistic ; and in either case it would have to be assumed that we were aware of what was true and what was false ; and it is seldom that we have any clear idea of the truth beforehand. The true conception of Dialectic is, then, that which we have formed : it is the art of intellectual fencing used for the purpose of getting the best of it in a dispute ; and, although the name *Eristic* would be more suitable, it is more correct to call it controversial Dialectic, *Dialectica eristica*.

Dialectic in this sense of the word has no other aim but to reduce to a regular system and collect and exhibit the arts which most men employ when they observe, in a dispute, that truth is not on their side, and still attempt to gain the day. Hence, it would be very inexpedient to pay any regard to objective truth or its advancement in a science of Dialectic; since this is not done in that original and natural Dialectic innate in men, where they strive for nothing but victory. The science of Dialectic, in one sense of the word, is mainly concerned to tabulate and analyse dishonest stratagems, in order that in a real debate they may be at once recognised and defeated. It is for this very reason that Dialectic must admittedly take victory, and not objective truth, for its aim and purpose.

I am not aware that anything has been done in this direction, although I have made inquiries far and wide.[1] It is, therefore, an uncultivated soil. To accomplish our purpose, we must draw from our experience ; we must observe how in the debates which often arise in our intercourse with our fellow-men this or that stratagem is employed by one side or the other. By finding out the common elements in tricks repeated in different forms, we shall be enabled to exhibit certain general stratagems which may be advantageous, as well for our own use, as for frustrating others if they use them.

What follows is to be regarded as a first attempt.

---

[1] Diogenes Laertes tells us that among the numerous writings on Rhetoric by Theophrastus, all of which have been lost, there was one entitled Ἀγωνιστικὸν τῆς περὶ τούς ἐριστικοὺς λόγους θεωρίας. That would have been just what we want.

THE BASIS OF ALL DIALECTIC.

First of all, we must consider the essential nature of every dispute : what it is that really takes place in it.

Our opponent has stated a thesis, or we ourselves, —it is all one. There are two modes of refuting it, and two courses that we may pursue.

I. The modes are (1) *ad rem*, (2) *ad hominem* or *ex concessis*. That is to say : We may show either that the proposition is not in accordance with the nature of things, *i.e.*, with absolute, objective truth ; or that it is inconsistent with other statements or admissions of our opponent, *i.e.*, with truth as it appears to him. The latter mode of arguing a question produces only a relative conviction, and makes no difference whatever to the objective truth of the matter.

II. The two courses that we may pursue are (1) the direct, and (2) the indirect refutation. The direct attacks the reason for the thesis ; the indirect, its results. The direct refutation shows that the thesis is not true ; the indirect, that it cannot be true.

The direct course admits of a twofold procedure. Either we may show that the reasons for the statement are false (*nego majorem, minorem*); or we may admit the reasons or premises, but show that the statement does not follow from them (*nego consequentiam*) ; that is, we attack the conclusion or form of the syllogism.

The direct refutation makes use either of the *diversion* or of the *instance*.

(*a*) The *diversion*.—We accept our opponent's pro-

position as true, and then show what follows from it
when we bring it into connection with some other
proposition acknowledged to be true. We use the two
propositions as the premisses of a syllogism giving a
conclusion which is manifestly false, as contradicting
either the nature of things,[1] or other statements of
our opponent himself; that is to say, the conclusion
is false either *ad rem* or *ad hominem*.[2] Consequently,
our opponent's proposition must have been false; for,
while true premisses can give only a true conclusion,
false premisses need not always give a false one.

(b) The *instance*, or the example to the contrary.
—This consists in refuting the general proposition by
direct reference to particular cases which are included
in it in the way in which it is stated, but to which it
does not apply, and by which it is therefore shown
to be necessarily false.

Such is the framework or skeleton of all forms of
disputation; for to this every kind of controversy
may be ultimately reduced. The whole of a controversy may, however, actually proceed in the
manner described, or only appear to do so; and it may
be supported by genuine or spurious arguments. It
is just because it is not easy to make out the truth
in regard to this matter, that debates are so long and
so obstinate.

Nor can we, in ordering the argument, separate
actual from apparent truth, since even the disputants
are not certain about it beforehand. Therefore I

---

[1] If it is in direct contradiction with a perfectly undoubted
truth, we have reduced our opponent's position *ad absurdum*.

[2] Socrates, in *Hippia Maj. et alias*.

shall describe the various tricks or stratagems without regard to questions of objective truth or falsity; for that is a matter on which we have no assurance, and which cannot be determined previously. Moreover, in every disputation or argument on any subject we must agree about something; and by this, as a principle, we must be willing to judge the matter in question. We cannot argue with those who deny principles: *Contra negantem principia non est disputandum.*

STRATAGEMS.

I.

The *Extension.*—This consists in carrying your opponent's proposition beyond its natural limits; in giving it as general a signification and as wide a sense as possible, so as to exaggerate it; and, on the other hand, in giving your own proposition as restricted a sense and as narrow limits as you can, because the more general a statement becomes, the more numerous are the objections to which it is open. The defence consists in an accurate statement of the point or essential question at issue.

Example 1. — I asserted that the English were supreme in drama. My opponent attempted to give an instance to the contrary, and replied that it was a well-known fact that in music, and consequently in opera, they could do nothing at all. I repelled the attack by reminding him that music was not included in dramatic art, which covered tragedy and comedy alone. This he knew very well. What he had done was to try

to generalise my proposition, so that it would apply
to all theatrical representations, and, consequently,
to opera and then to music, in order to make certain
of defeating me.   Contrarily, we may save our proposition by reducing it within narrower limits than
we had first intended, if our way of expressing it
favours this expedient.

Example 2.—A. declares that the Peace of 1814
gave back their independence to all the German towns
of the Hanseatic League.   B. gives an instance to the
contrary by reciting the fact that Dantzig, which
received its independence from Buonaparte, lost it by
that Peace.   A. saves himself thus : " I said ' all
German towns,' and Dantzig was in Poland ".

This trick was mentioned by Aristotle in the *Topica* (bk. viii., cc. 11, 12).

Example 3.—Lamarck, in his *Philosophie Zoologique*
(vol. i., p. 203), states that the polype has no feeling,
because it has no nerves.   It is certain, however, that
it has some sort of perception ; for it advances towards
light by moving in an ingenious fashion from branch
to branch, and it seizes its prey.   Hence it has been
assumed that its nervous system is spread over the
whole of its body in equal measure, as though it were
blended with it ; for it is obvious that the polype
possesses some faculty of perception without having
any separate organs of sense.   Since this assumption
refutes Lamarck's position, he argues thus : " In that
case all parts of its body must be capable of every
kind of feeling, and also of motion, of will, of thought.
The polype would have all the organs of the most
perfect animal in every point of its body ; every

point could see, smell, taste, hear, and so on; nay, it could think, judge, and draw conclusions; every particle of its body would be a perfect animal, and it would stand higher than man, as every part of it would possess all the faculties which man possesses only in the whole of him. Further, there would be no reason for not extending what is true of the polype to all monads, the most imperfect of all creatures, and ultimately to the plants, which are also alive, etc., etc." By using dialectical tricks of this kind a writer betrays that he is secretly conscious of being in the wrong. Because it was said that the creature's whole body is sensitive to light, and is therefore possessed of nerves, he makes out that its whole body is capable of thought.

II.

The *Homonymy.*—This trick is to extend a proposition to something which has little or nothing in common with the matter in question but the similarity of the word; then to refute it triumphantly, and so claim credit for having refuted the original statement.

It may be noted here that synonyms are two words for the same conception; homonyms, two conceptions which are covered by the same word. (See Aristotle, *Topica*, bk. i., c. 13.) "Deep," "cutting," "high," used at one moment of bodies, at another of tones, are homonyms; "honourable" and "honest" are synonyms.

This is a trick which may be regarded as identical

with the sophism *ex homonymia;* although, if the sophism is obvious, it will deceive no one.

Every light can be extinguished.
The intellect is a light.
Therefore it can be extinguished.

Here it is at once clear that there are four terms in the syllogism, "light" being used both in a real and in a metaphorical sense. But if the sophism takes a subtle form, it is, of course, apt to mislead, especially where the conceptions which are covered by the same word are related, and inclined to be interchangeable. It is never subtle enough to deceive, if it is used intentionally; and therefore cases of it must be collected from actual and individual experience.

It would be a very good thing if every trick could receive some short and obviously appropriate name, so that when a man used this or that particular trick, he could be at once reproached for it.

I will give two examples of the homonymy.

Example 1.—A.: "You are not yet initiated into the mysteries of the Kantian philosophy."

B.: "Oh, if it's mysteries you're talking of, I'll have nothing to do with them."

Example 2.—I condemned the principle involved in the word *honour* as a foolish one; for, according to it, a man loses his honour by receiving an insult, which he cannot wipe out unless he replies with a still greater insult, or by shedding his adversary's blood or his own. I contended that a man's true honour cannot be outraged by what he suffers, but only and alone by what he does; for there is no saying what may befall any one of us. My opponent immediately attacked the reason I had given, and triumphantly proved to me that when a tradesman was falsely accused of misrepresentation, dishonesty, or neglect in his business, it was an attack upon his honour. which in this case was outraged solely by what he suffered, and that he could only retrieve it by punishing his aggressor and making him retract.

Here, by a homonymy, he was foisting *civic honour*, which is otherwise called *good name*, and which may be outraged by libel and slander, on to the conception of *knightly honour*, also called *point d'honneur*, which may be outraged by insult. And since an attack on the former cannot be disregarded, but must be repelled by public disproof, so, with the same justification, an attack on the latter must not be disregarded either, but it must be defeated by still greater insult and a duel. Here we have a confusion of two essentially different things through the homonymy in the word *honour*, and a consequent alteration of the point in dispute.

III.

Another trick is to take a proposition which is laid down relatively, and in reference to some particular matter, as though it were uttered with a general or absolute application; or, at least, to take it in some quite different sense, and then refute it. Aristotle's example is as follows:—

A Moor is black; but in regard to his teeth he is white; therefore, he is black and not black at the same moment. This is an obvious sophism, which will deceive no one. Let us contrast it with one drawn from actual experience.

In talking of philosophy, I admitted that my system upheld the Quietists, and commended them. Shortly afterwards the conversation turned upon Hegel, and I maintained that his writings were mostly nonsense; or, at any rate, that there were many passages in them where the author wrote the words, and it was left to the reader to find a meaning for them. My opponent did not attempt to refute this assertion *ad rem,* but contented himself by advancing the *argumentum ad hominem,* and telling me that I had just been praising the Quietists, and that they had written a good deal of nonsense too.

This I admitted; but, by way of correcting him, I said that I had praised the Quietists, not as philosophers and writers, that is to say, for their achievements in the sphere of *theory,* but only as men, and for their conduct in mere matters of *practice;* and that in Hegel's case we were talking of theories. In this way I parried the attack.

The first three tricks are of a kindred character. They have this in common, that something different is attacked from that which was asserted. It would therefore be an *ignoratio elenchi* to allow oneself to be disposed of in such a manner.

For in all the examples that I have given, what the opponent says is true, but it stands in apparent and not in real contradiction with the thesis. All that the man whom he is attacking has to do is to deny the validity of his syllogism; to deny, namely, the conclusion which he draws, that because his proposition is true, ours is false. In this way his refutation is itself directly refuted by a denial of his conclusion, *per negationem consequentiae.* Another trick is to refuse to admit true premisses because of a foreseen conclusion. There are two ways of defeating it, incorporated in the next two sections.

IV.

If you want to draw a conclusion, you must not let it be foreseen, but you must get the premisses admitted one by one, unobserved, mingling them here and there in your talk; otherwise, your opponent will attempt all sorts of chicanery. Or, if it is doubtful whether your opponent will admit them, you must advance the premisses of these premisses; that is to say, you must draw up pro-syllogisms, and get the premisses of several of them admitted in no definite order. In this way you conceal your game until you have obtained all the admissions that are necessary, and so reach your goal by making a circuit. These rules are given by Aristotle in his *Topica*, bk. viii. c. 1. It is a trick which needs no illustration.

V.

To prove the truth of a proposition, you may also employ previous propositions that are not true, should your opponent refuse to admit the true ones, either because he fails to perceive their truth, or because he sees that the thesis immediately follows from them. In that case the plan is to take propositions which are false in themselves but true for your opponent, and argue from the way in which he thinks, that is to say, *ex concessis*. For a true conclusion may follow from false premisses, but not *vice versâ*. In the same fashion your opponent's false propositions may be refuted by other false propositions, which he, however, takes to be true; for it is with him that you have to do, and you must use the thoughts that he uses. For instance, if he is a member of some sect to which you do not belong, you may employ the declared opinions of this sect against him, as principles.[1]

VI.

Another plan is to beg the question in disguise by postulating what has to be proved, either (1) under another name; for instance, "good repute" instead of "honour"; "virtue" instead of "virginity," etc.; or by using such convertible terms as "red-blooded animals" and "vertebrates"; or (2) by making a general assumption covering the particular point in dispute; for instance, maintaining the uncertainty of medicine by postulating the uncertainty of all human knowledge. (3) If, *vice versâ*, two things follow one from the other, and one is to be proved, you may postulate the other. (4) If a general proposition is to be proved, you may get your opponent to admit every one of the particulars. This is the converse of the second.[2]

[1] Aristotle, *Topica*, bk. viii., chap. 2.

[2] *Idem*, chap. 11. The last chapter of this work contains some good rules for the practice of Dialectics.

VII.

Should the disputation be conducted on somewhat strict and formal lines, and there be a desire to arrive at a very clear understanding, he who states the proposition and wants to prove it may proceed against his opponent by question, in order to show the truth of the statement from his admissions. This erotematic, or Socratic, method was especially in use among the ancients; and this and some of the tricks following later on are akin to it.[1]

The plan is to ask a great many wide-reaching questions at once, so as to hide what you want to get admitted, and, on the other hand, quickly propound the argument resulting from the admissions; for those who are slow of understanding cannot follow accurately, and do not notice any mistakes or gaps there may be in the demonstration.

VIII.

This trick consists in making your opponent angry; for when he is angry he is incapable of judging aright, and perceiving where his advantage lies. You can make him angry by doing him repeated injustice, or practising some kind of chicanery, and being generally insolent.

IX.

Or you may put questions in an order different from that which the conclusion to be drawn from

[1] They are all a free version of chap. 15 of Aristotle's *De Sophistici Elenchis*.

them requires, and transpose them, so as not to let him know at what you are aiming. He can then take no precautions. You may also use his answers for different or even opposite conclusions, according to their character. This is akin to the trick of masking your procedure.

X.

If you observe that your opponent designedly returns a negative answer to the questions which, for the sake of your proposition, you want him to answer in the affirmative, you must ask the converse of the proposition, as though it were that which you were anxious to see affirmed ; or, at any rate, you may give him his choice of both, so that he may not perceive which of them you are asking him to affirm.

XI.

If you make an induction, and your opponent grants you the particular cases by which it is to be supported, you must refrain from asking him if he also admits the general truth which issues from the particulars, but introduce it afterwards as a settled and admitted fact ; for, in the meanwhile, he will himself come to believe that he has admitted it, and the same impression will be received by the audience, because they will remember the many questions as to the particulars, and suppose that they must, of course, have attained their end.

XII.

If the conversation turns upon some general conception which has no particular name, but requires some figurative or metaphorical designation, you must begin by choosing a metaphor that is favourable to your proposition. For instance, the names used to denote the two political parties in Spain, *Serviles* and *Liberales*, are obviously chosen by the latter. The name *Protestants* is chosen by themselves, and also the name *Evangelicals;* but the Catholics call them *heretics*. Similarly, in regard to the names of things which admit of a more exact and definite meaning: for example, if your opponent proposes an *alteration*, you can call it an *innovation*, as this is an invidious word. If you yourself make the proposal, it will be the converse. In the first case, you can call the antagonistic principle "the existing order," in the second, "antiquated prejudice". What an impartial man with no further purpose to serve would call "public worship" or a "system of religion," is described by an adherent as "piety," "godliness"; and by an opponent as "bigotry," "superstition". This is, at bottom, a subtle *petitio principii*. What is sought to be proved is, first of all, inserted in the definition, whence it is then taken by mere analysis. What one man calls "placing in safe custody," another calls "throwing into prison". A speaker often betrays his purpose beforehand by the names which he gives to things. One man talks of "the clergy"; another, of "the priests".

Of all the tricks of controversy, this is the most frequent, and it is used instinctively. You hear of "religious zeal," or "fanaticism"; a "*faux pas*," a "piece of gallantry," or "adultery"; an "equivocal," or a "bawdy" story; "embarrassment," or "bankruptcy";

"through influence and connection," or by "bribery and nepotism"; "sincere gratitude," or "good pay".

XIII.

To make your opponent accept a proposition, you must give him the counter-proposition as well, leaving him his choice of the two; and you must render the contrast as glaring as you can, so that to avoid being paradoxical he will accept the proposition, which is thus made to look quite probable. For instance, if you want to make him admit that a boy must do everything that his father tells him to do, ask him "whether in all things we must obey or disobey our parents". Or, if a thing is said to occur "often," ask whether by "often" you are to understand few or many cases; and he will say "many". It is as though you were to put grey next black, and call it white; or next white, and call it black.

XIV.

This, which is an impudent trick, is played as follows: When your opponent has answered several of your questions without the answers turning out favourable to the conclusion at which you are aiming, advance the desired conclusion,—although it does not in the least follow,—as though it had been proved, and proclaim it in a tone of triumph. If your opponent is shy or stupid, and you yourself possess a great deal of impudence and a good voice, the trick may easily succeed. It is akin to the fallacy *non causae ut causae.*

XV.

If you have advanced a paradoxical proposition and find a difficulty in proving it, you may submit for your opponent's acceptance or rejection some true proposition, the truth of which, however, is not quite palpable, as though you wished to draw your proof from it. Should he reject it because he suspects a trick, you can obtain your triumph by showing how absurd he is ; should he accept it, you have got reason on your side for the moment, and must now look about you ; or else you can employ the previous trick as well, and maintain that your paradox is proved by the proposition which he has accepted. For this an extreme degree of impudence is required ; but experience shows cases of it, and there are people who practise it by instinct.

XVI.

Another trick is to use arguments *ad hominem*, or *ex concessis.*[1] When your opponent makes a

[1] The truth from which I draw my proof may be either (1) of an objective and universally valid character ; in that case my proof is veracious, *secundum veritatem :* and it is such proof alone that has any genuine validity. Or (2) it may be valid only for the person to whom I wish to prove my proposition, and with whom I am disputing. He has, that is to say, either taken up some position once for all as a prejudice, or hastily admitted it in the course of the dispute ; and on this I ground my proof. In that case, it is a proof valid only for this particular man, *ad hominem.* I compel my opponent to grant my proposition, but I fail to establish it as a truth of universal validity. My proof avails for my opponent alone, but for no one else. For example, if my opponent is a

proposition, you must try to see whether it is not in some way — if needs be, only apparently — inconsistent with some other proposition which he has made or admitted, or with the principles of a school or sect which he has commended and approved, or with the actions of those who support the sect, or else of those who give it only an apparent and spurious support, or with his own actions or want of action. For example, should he defend suicide, you may at once exclaim, "Why don't you hang yourself?" Should he maintain that Berlin is an unpleasant place to live in, you may say, "Why don't you leave by the first train?" Some such claptrap is always possible.

XVII.

If your opponent presses you with a counter-proof, you will often be able to save yourself by advancing some subtle distinction, which, it is true, had not previously occurred to you; that is, if the matter admits of a double application, or of being taken in any ambiguous sense.

XVIII.

If you observe that your opponent has taken up a line of argument which will end in your defeat, you

devotee of Kant's, and I ground my proof on some utterance of that philosopher, it is a proof which in itself is only *ad hominem*. If he is a Mohammedan, I may prove my point by reference to a passage in the Koran, and that is sufficient for him; but here it is only a proof *ad hominem*.

must not allow him to carry it to its conclusion, but interrupt the course of the dispute in time, or break it off altogether, or lead him away from the subject, and bring him to others. In short, you must effect the trick which will be noticed later on, the *mutatio controversiae*. (See § xxix.)

XIX.

Should your opponent expressly challenge you to produce any objection to some definite point in his argument, and you have nothing much to say, you must try to give the matter a general turn, and then talk against that. If you are called upon to say why a particular physical hypothesis cannot be accepted, you may speak of the fallibility of human knowledge, and give various illustrations of it.

XX.

When you have elicited all your premisses, and your opponent has admitted them, you must refrain from asking him for the conclusion, but draw it at once for yourself; nay, even though one or other of the premisses should be lacking, you may take it as though it too had been admitted, and draw the conclusion. This trick is an application of the fallacy *non causae ut causae*.

XXI.

When your opponent uses a merely superficial or sophistical argument and you see through it, you can, it is true, refute it by setting forth its captious and superficial character; but it is better to meet him with a counter-argument which is just as superficial and sophistical, and so dispose of him; for it is with victory that you are concerned, and not with truth. If, for example, he adopts an *argumentum ad hominem*, it is sufficient to take the force out of it by a counter *argumentum ad hominem* or *argumentum ex concessis*; and, in general, instead of setting forth the true state of the case at equal length, it is shorter to take this course if it lies open to you.

XXII.

If your opponent requires you to admit something from which the point in dispute will immediately follow, you must refuse to do so, declaring that it is a *petitio principii*. For he and the audience will regard a proposition which is near akin to the point in dispute as identical with it, and in this way you deprive him of his best argument.

XXIII.

Contradiction and contention irritate a man into exaggerating his statement. By contradicting your opponent you may drive him into extending beyond its proper limits a statement which, at all events within those limits and in itself, is true; and when you refute this exaggerated form of it, you look as though you had also refuted his original statement. Contrarily, you must take care not to allow yourself to be misled by contradiction into exaggerating or extending a statement of your own. It will often happen that your opponent will himself directly try to extend your statement further than you meant it; here you must at once stop him, and bring him back to the limits which you set up: "That's what I said, and no more".

XXIV.

This trick consists in stating a false syllogism. Your opponent makes a proposition, and by false inference and distortion of his ideas you force from it other propositions which it does not contain and he does not in the least mean; nay, which are absurd or dangerous. It then looks as if his proposition gave rise to others which are inconsistent either with themselves or with some acknowledged truth, and so it appears to be indirectly refuted. This is the *diversion*, and it is another application of the fallacy *non causae ut causae*.

XXV.

This is a case of the *diversion* by means of an *instance to the contrary*. With an induction (ἐπαγωγή), a great number of particular instances are required in order to establish it as a universal proposition; but with the *diversion* (ἀπαγωγή) a single instance, to which the proposition does not apply, is all that is necessary to overthrow it. This is a controversial method known as the *instance—instantia*, ἔνστασις. For example, "all ruminants are horned" is a proposition which may be upset by the single instance of the camel. The *instance* is a case in which a universal truth is sought to be applied, and something is inserted in the fundamental definition of it which is not universally true, and by which it is upset. But there is room for mistake; and when this trick is employed by your opponent, you must observe (1) whether the example which he gives is really true; for there are problems of which the only true solution is that the case in point is not true—for example, many miracles, ghost stories, and so on; and (2) whether it really comes under the conception of the truth thus stated; for it may only appear to do so and the matter is one to be settled by precise distinctions; and (3) whether it is really inconsistent with this conception; for this again may be only an apparent inconsistency.

XXVI.

A brilliant move is the *retorsio argumenti*, or turning of the tables, by which your opponent's argument is turned against himself. He declares, for instance, "So-and-so is a child, you must make allowance for him". You retort, "Just because he is a child, I must correct him otherwise he will persist in his bad habits ".

XXVII.

Should your opponent surprise you by becoming particularly angry at an argument, you must urge it with all the more zeal; not only because it is a good thing to make him angry, but because it may be presumed that you have here put your finger on the weak side of his case, and that just here he is more open to attack than even for the moment you perceive.

XXVIII.

This is chiefly practicable in a dispute between scholars in the presence of the unlearned. If you have no argument *ad rem*, and none either *ad hominem*, you can make one *ad auditores*; that is to say, you can start some invalid objection, which, however, only an expert sees to be invalid. Now your opponent is an expert, but those who form your audience are not, and accordingly in their eyes he is defeated; particularly if the objection which you make places him in any ridiculous light. People are ready to laugh, and you have the laughers on your side. To show that your objection is an idle one, would require a long explanation on the part of your opponent, and a reference to the principles of the branch of knowledge in question, or to the elements of the matter which you are discussing: and people are not disposed to listen to it.

For example, your opponent states that in the original formation of a mountain-range the granite and other elements in its composition were, by reason of their high temperature, in a fluid or molten state; that the temperature must have amounted to some 480° Fahrenheit; and that when the mass took shape it was covered by the sea. You reply, by an argument *ad auditores*, that at that temperature—nay, indeed, long before it had been reached, namely, at 212° Fahrenheit—the sea would have been boiled away, and spread through the air in the form of steam. At this the audience laughs. To refute the objection, your opponent would have to show that the boiling-point depends not only on the degree of warmth, but also on the atmospheric pressure; and that as soon as about half the sea-water had gone off in the shape of steam, this pressure would be so greatly increased that the rest of it would fail to boil even at a temperature of 480°. He is debarred from giving this explanation, as it would require a treatise to demonstrate the matter to those who had no acquaintance with physics.

XXIX. [1]

If you find that you are being worsted, you can make a *diversion*—that is, you can suddenly begin to talk of something else, as though it had a bearing on the matter in dispute, and afforded an argument against your opponent. This may be done without presumption if the diversion has, in fact, some general bearing on the matter; but it is a piece of impudence if it has nothing to do with the case, and is only brought in by way of attacking your opponent.

For example, I praised the system prevailing in China, where there is no such thing as hereditary nobility, and offices are bestowed only on those who succeed in competitive examinations. My opponent maintained that learning, as little as the

[1] See § xviii.

privilege of birth (of which he had a high opinion), fits a man for office. We argued, and he got the worst of it. Then he made a diversion, and declared that in China all ranks were punished with the bastinado, which he connected with the immoderate indulgence in tea, and proceeded to make both of them a subject of reproach to the Chinese. To follow him into all this would have been to allow oneself to be drawn into a surrender of the victory which had already been won.

The diversion is mere impudence if it completely abandons the point in dispute, and raises, for instance, some such objection as " Yes, and you also said just now," and so on. For then the argument becomes to some extent personal; of the kind which will be treated of in the last section. Strictly speaking, it is half-way between the *argumentum ad personam*, which will there be discussed, and the *argumentum ad hominem.*

How very innate this trick is, may be seen in every quarrel between common people. If one of the parties makes some personal reproach against the other, the latter, instead of answering it by refuting it, allows it to stand,—as it were, admits it; and replies by reproaching his antagonist on some other ground. This is a stratagem like that pursued by Scipio when he attacked the Carthaginians, not in Italy, but in Africa. In war, diversions of this kind may be profitable; but in a quarrel they are poor expedients, because the reproaches remain, and those who look on hear the worst that can be said of both parties. It is a trick that should be used only *faute de mieux.*

XXX.

This is the *argumentum ad verecundiam*. It consists in making an appeal to authority rather than reason, and in using such an authority as may suit the degree of knowledge possessed by your opponent.

Every man prefers belief to the exercise of judgment, says Seneca ; and it is therefore an easy matter if you have an authority on your side which your opponent respects. The more limited his capacity and knowledge, the greater is the number of the authorities who weigh with him. But if his capacity and knowledge are of a high order, there are very few ; indeed, hardly any at all. He may, perhaps, admit the authority of professional men versed in a science or an art or a handicraft of which he knows little or nothing ; but even so he will regard it with suspicion. Contrarily, ordinary folk have a deep respect for professional men of every kind. They are unaware that a man who makes a profession of a thing loves it not for the thing itself, but for the money he makes by it ; or that it is rare for a man who teaches to know his subject thoroughly ; for if he studies it as he ought, he has in most cases no time left in which to teach it.

But there are very many authorities who find respect with the mob, and if you have none that is quite suitable, you can take one that appears to be so ; you may quote what some said in another sense or in other circumstances. Authorities which your opponent fails to understand are those of which he generally thinks the most. The unlearned entertain a peculiar respect for a Greek or a Latin flourish.

You may also, should it be necessary, not only twist your authorities, but actually falsify them, or quote something which you have invented entirely yourself. As a rule, your opponent has no books at hand, and could not use them if he had. The finest illustration of this is furnished by the French *curé*, who, to avoid being compelled, like other citizens, to pave the street in front of his house, quoted a saying which he described as biblical: *paveant illi, ego non pavebo.* That was quite enough for the municipal officers.

A universal prejudice may also be used as an authority; for most people think with Aristotle that that may be said to exist which many believe. There is no opinion, however absurd, which men will not readily embrace as soon as they can be brought to the conviction that it is generally adopted. Example affects their thought just as it affects their action. They are like sheep following the bell-wether just as he leads them. They would sooner die than think. It is very curious that the universality of an opinion should have so much weight with people, as their own experience might tell them that its acceptance is an entirely thoughtless and merely imitative process. But it tells them nothing of the kind, because they possess no self-knowledge whatever. It is only the elect who say with Plato: τοῖς πολλοῖς πολλὰ δοκεῖ; which means that the public has a good many bees in its bonnet, and that it would be a long business to get at them.

But to speak seriously, the universality of an opinion is no proof, nay, it is not even a probability, that the opinion is right. Those who maintain that it

is so must assume (1) that length of time deprives a
universal opinion of its demonstrative force, as otherwise all the old errors which were once universally
held to be true would have to be recalled; for instance,
the Ptolemaic system would have to be restored, or
Catholicism re-established in all Protestant countries.
They must assume (2) that distance of space has the
same effect; otherwise the respective universality of
opinion among the adherents of Buddhism, Chris-
tianity, and Islam will put them in a difficulty.

When we come to look into the matter, so-called
universal opinion is the opinion of two or three persons; and we should be persuaded of this if we could
see the way in which it really arises.

We should find that it is two or three persons who,
in the first instance, accepted it, or advanced and
maintained it; and of whom people were so good as to
believe that they had thoroughly tested it. Then a
few other persons, persuaded beforehand that the
first were men of the requisite capacity, also accepted
the opinion. These, again, were trusted by many
others, whose laziness suggested to them that it was
better to believe at once, than to go through the
troublesome task of testing the matter for themselves.
Thus the number of these lazy and credulous adherents grew from day to day; for the opinion had
no sooner obtained a fair measure of support than its
further supporters attributed this to the fact that the
opinion could only have obtained it by the cogency of
its arguments. The remainder were then compelled
to grant what was universally granted, so as not to
pass for unruly persons who resisted opinions which

every one accepted, or pert fellows who thought themselves cleverer than any one else.

When opinion reaches this stage, adhesion becomes a duty; and henceforward the few who are capable of forming a judgment hold their peace. Those who venture to speak are such as are entirely incapable of forming any opinions or any judgment of their own, being merely the echo of others' opinions; and, nevertheless, they defend them with all the greater zeal and intolerance. For what they hate in people who think differently is not so much the different opinions which they profess, as the presumption of wanting to form their own judgment; a presumption of which they themselves are never guilty, as they are very well aware. In short, there are very few who can think, but every man wants to have an opinion; and what remains but to take it ready-made from others, instead of forming opinions for himself?

Since this is what happens, where is the value of the opinion even of a hundred millions? It is no more established than an historical fact reported by a hundred chroniclers who can be proved to have plagiarised it from one another; the opinion in the end being traceable to a single individual.[1] It is all what I say, what you say, and, finally, what he says; and the whole of it is nothing but a series of assertions:—

Dico ego, tu dicis, sed denique dixit et ille;
Dictaque post toties, nil nisi dicta vides.

Nevertheless, in a dispute with ordinary people, we may employ universal opinion as an authority. For

[1] See Bayle's *Pensées sur les Comètes*, i., p. 10.

it will generally be found that when two of them are
fighting, that is the weapon which both of them
choose as a means of attack. If a man of the better
sort has to deal with them, it is most advisable for
him to condescend to the use of this weapon too, and
to select such authorities as will make an impression
on his opponent's weak side. For, *ex hypothesi*, he is
as insensible to all rational argument as a horny-
hided Siegfried, dipped in the flood of incapacity, and
unable to think or judge.

Before a tribunal the dispute is one between authorities alone,—such authoritative statements, I mean, as
are laid down by legal experts; and here the exercise
of judgment consists in discovering what law or
authority applies to the case in question. There is,
however, plenty of room for Dialectic; for should the
case in question and the law not really fit each other,
they can, if necessary, be twisted until they appear
to do so, or *vice versá*.

XXXI.

If you know that you have no reply to the arguments
which your opponent advances, you may, by a fine
stroke of irony, declare yourself to be an incompetent
judge: "What you now say passes my poor powers of
comprehension; it may be all very true, but I can't
understand it, and I refrain from any expression of
opinion on it". In this way you insinuate to the bystanders, with whom you are in good repute, that
what your opponent says is nonsense. Thus, when
Kant's *Kritik* appeared, or, rather, when it began to

make a noise in the world, many professors of the old eclectic school declared that they failed to understand it, in the belief that their failure settled the business. But when the adherents of the new school proved to them that they were quite right, and had really failed to understand it, they were in a very bad humour.

This is a trick which may be used only when you are quite sure that the audience thinks much better of you than of your opponent. A professor, for instance, may try it on a student.

Strictly, it is a case of the preceding trick : it is a particularly malicious assertion of one's own authority, instead of giving reasons. The counter-trick is to say : " I beg your pardon ; but, with your penetrating intellect, it must be very easy for you to understand anything ; and it can only be my poor statement of the matter that is at fault "; and then go on to rub it into him until he understands it *nolens volens*, and sees for himself that it was really his own fault alone. In this way you parry his attack. With the greatest politeness he wanted to insinuate that you were talking nonsense ; and you, with equal courtesy, prove to him that he is a fool.

XXXII.

If you are confronted with an assertion, there is a short way of getting rid of it, or, at any rate, of throwing suspicion on it, by putting it into some odious category ; even though the connection is only apparent, or else of a loose character. You can say, for in-

stance, " That is Manichæism," or " It is Arianism," or
" Pelagianism," or " Idealism," or " Spinozism," or
" Pantheism," or " Brownianism," or " Naturalism," or
" Atheism," or " Rationalism," " Spiritualism," " Mysticism," and so on. In making an objection of this kind,
you take it for granted (1) that the assertion in
question is identical with, or is at least contained in,
the category cited—that is to say, you cry out, " Oh,
I have heard that before "; and (2) that the system
referred to has been entirely refuted, and does not
contain a word of truth.

XXXIII.

" That's all very well in theory, but it won't do in
practice." In this sophism you admit the premises
but deny the conclusion, in contradiction with a well-
known rule of logic. The assertion is based upon an
impossibility : what is right in theory *must* work in
practice ; and if it does not, there is a mistake in the
theory ; something has been overlooked and not
allowed for ; and, consequently, what is wrong in
practice is wrong in theory too.

XXXIV.

When you state a question or an argument, and
your opponent gives you no direct answer or reply,
but evades it by a counter-question or an indirect
answer, or some assertion which has no bearing on
the matter, and, generally, tries to turn the subject,
it is a sure sign that you have touched a weak
spot, sometimes without knowing it. You have, as it

were, reduced him to silence. You must, therefore, urge the point all the more, and not let your opponent evade it, even when you do not know where the weakness which you have hit upon really lies.

XXXV.

There is another trick which, as soon as it is practicable, makes all others unnecessary. Instead of working on your opponent's intellect by argument, work on his will by motive; and he, and also the audience if they have similar interests, will at once be won over to your opinion, even though you got it out of a lunatic asylum; for, as a general rule, half an ounce of will is more effective than a hundred-weight of insight and intelligence. This, it is true, can be done only under peculiar circumstances. If you succeed in making your opponent feel that his opinion, should it prove true, will be distinctly prejudicial to his interest, he will let it drop like a hot potato, and feel that it was very imprudent to take it up.

A clergyman, for instance, is defending some philosophical dogma; you make him sensible of the fact that it is in immediate contradiction with one of the fundamental doctrines of his Church, and he abandons it.

A landed proprietor maintains that the use of machinery in agricultural operations, as practised in England, is an excellent institution, since an engine does the work of many men. You give him to understand that it will not be very long before carriages are also worked by steam, and that the value of his large stud will be greatly depreciated; and you will see what he will say.

In such cases every man feels how thoughtless it is to sanction a law unjust to himself—*quam temere in nosmet legem sancimus iniquam!* Nor is it otherwise if the bystanders, but not your opponent, belong to the same sect, guild, industry, club, etc., as yourself. Let his thesis be never so true, as soon as you hint that it is prejudicial to the common interests of the said society, all the bystanders will find that your opponent's arguments, however excellent they be, are weak and contemptible; and that yours, on the other hand, though they were random conjecture, are correct and to the point; you will have a chorus of loud approval on your side, and your opponent will be driven out of the field with ignominy. Nay, the bystanders will believe, as a rule, that they have agreed with you out of pure conviction. For what is not to our interest mostly seems absurd to us; our intellect being no *siccum lumen*. This trick might be called "taking the tree by its root"; its usual name is the *argumentum ab utili*.

XXXVI.

You may also puzzle and bewilder your opponent by mere bombast; and the trick is possible, because a man generally supposes that there must be some meaning in words :—

> *Gewöhnlich glaubt der Mensch, wenn er nur Worte hört,*
> *Es müsse sich dabei doch auch was denken lassen.*

If he is secretly conscious of his own weakness, and

accustomed to hear much that he does not understand, and to make as though he did, you can easily impose upon him by some serious fooling that sounds very deep or learned, and deprives him of hearing, sight, and thought ; and by giving out that it is the most indisputable proof of what you assert. It is a well-known fact that in recent times some philosophers have practised this trick on the whole of the public with the most brilliant success. But since present examples are odious, we may refer to *The Vicar of Wakefield* for an old one.

XXXVII.

Should your opponent be in the right, but, luckily for your contention, choose a faulty proof, you can easily manage to refute it, and then claim that you have thus refuted his whole position. This is a trick which ought to be one of the first; it is, at bottom, an expedient by which an *argumentum ad hominem* is put forward as an *argumentum ad rem*. If no accurate proof occurs to him or to the bystanders, you have won the day. For example, if a man advances the ontological argument by way of proving God's existence, you can get the best of him, for the ontological argument may easily be refuted. This is the way in which bad advocates lose a good case, by trying to justify it by an authority which does not fit it, when no fitting one occurs to them.

XXXVIII.

A last trick is to become personal, insulting, rude,

as soon as you perceive that your opponent has the upper hand, and that you are going to come off worst. It consists in passing from the subject of dispute, as from a lost game, to the disputant himself, and in some way attacking his person. It may be called the *argumentum ad personam,* to distinguish it from the *argumentum ad hominem,* which passes from the objective discussion of the subject pure and simple to the statements or admissions which your opponent has made in regard to it. But in becoming personal you leave the subject altogether, and turn your attack to his person, by remarks of an offensive and spiteful character. It is an appeal from the virtues of the intellect to the virtues of the body, or to mere animalism. This is a very popular trick, because every one is able to carry it into effect; and so it is of frequent application. Now the question is, What counter-trick avails for the other party? for if he has recourse to the same rule, there will be blows, or a duel, or an action for slander.

It would be a great mistake to suppose that it is sufficient not to become personal yourself. For by showing a man quite quietly that he is wrong, and that what he says and thinks is incorrect—a process which occurs in every dialectical victory—you embitter him more than if you used some rude or insulting expression. Why is this? Because, as Hobbes observes,[1] all mental pleasure consists in being able to compare oneself with others to one's own advantage. Nothing is of greater moment to a man than the gratification of his vanity, and no

[1] *Elementa philosophica de Cive.*

wound is more painful than that which is inflicted on it. Hence such phrases as "Death before dishonour," and so on. The gratification of vanity arises mainly by comparison of oneself with others, in every respect, but chiefly in respect of one's intellectual powers; and so the most effective and the strongest gratification of it is to be found in controversy. Hence the embitterment of defeat, apart from any question of injustice; and hence recourse to that last weapon, that last trick, which you cannot evade by mere politeness. A cool demeanour may, however, help you here, if, as soon as your opponent becomes personal, you quietly reply, "That has no bearing on the point in dispute," and immediately bring the conversation back to it, and continue to show him that he is wrong, without taking any notice of his insults. Say, as Themistocles said to Eurybiades—*Strike, but hear me.* But such demeanour is not given to every one.

As a sharpening of wits, controversy is often, indeed, of mutual advantage, in order to correct one's thoughts and awaken new views. But in learning and in mental power both disputants must be tolerably equal. If one of them lacks learning, he will fail to understand the other, as he is not on the same level with his antagonist. If he lacks mental power, he will be embittered, and led into dishonest tricks, and end by being rude.

The only safe rule, therefore, is that which Aristotle mentions in the last chapter of his *Topica :* not to dispute with the first person you meet, but only with those of your acquaintance of whom you know that

they possess sufficient intelligence and self-
not to advance absurdities; to appeal to reaso
not to authority, and to listen to reason and yiel
and, finally, to cherish truth, to be willing to
reason even from an opponent, and to be just e
to bear being proved to be in the wrong, should
lie with him. From this it follows that scarce
man in a hundred is worth your disputing wit
You may let the remainder say what they plea
every one is at liberty to be a fool—*desipere e
gentium*. Remember what Voltaire says : *La
vaut encore mieux que la vérité*. Remember a
Arabian proverb which tells us that *on the t
silence there hangs its fruit, which is peace.*

ON THE COMPARATIVE PLACE OF INTE
AND BEAUTY IN WORKS OF ART.

ON THE COMPARATIVE PLACE OF INTEREST AND BEAUTY IN WORKS OF ART.

In the productions of poetic genius, especially of the epic and dramatic kind, there is, apart from Beauty, another quality which is attractive: I mean Interest.

The beauty of a work of art consists in the fact that it holds up a clear mirror to certain *ideas* inherent in the world in general; the beauty of a work of poetic art in particular is that it renders the ideas inherent in mankind, and thereby leads it to a knowledge of these ideas. The means which poetry uses for this end are the exhibition of significant characters and the invention of circumstances which will bring about significant situations, giving occasion to the characters to unfold their peculiarities and show what is in them; so that by some such representation a clearer and fuller knowledge of the many-sided idea of humanity may be attained. Beauty, however, in its general aspect, is the inseparable characteristic of the idea when it has become known. In other words, everything is beautiful in which an idea is revealed; for to be beautiful means no more than clearly to express an idea.

Thus we perceive that beauty is always an affair of *knowledge*, and that it appeals to *the knowing subject*, and not to *the will ;* nay, it is a fact that the apprehension of beauty on the part of the subject involves a complete suppression of the will.

On the other hand, we call drama or descriptive poetry interesting when it represents events and actions of a kind which necessarily arouse concern or sympathy, like that which we feel in real events involving our own person. The fate of the person represented in them is felt in just the same fashion as our own : we await the development of events with anxiety ; we eagerly follow their course ; our hearts quicken when the hero is threatened ; our pulse falters as the danger reaches its acme, and throbs again when he is suddenly rescued. Until we reach the end of the story we cannot put the book aside ; we lie awake far into the night sympathising with our hero's troubles as though they were our own. Nay, instead of finding pleasure and recreation in such representations, we should feel all the pain which real life often inflicts upon us, or at least the kind which pursues us in our uneasy dreams, if in the act of reading or looking at the stage we had not the firm ground of reality always beneath our feet. As it is, in the stress of a too violent feeling, we can find relief from the illusion of the moment, and then give way to it again at will. Moreover, we can gain this relief without any such violent transition as occurs in a dream, when we rid ourselves of its terrors only by the act of awaking.

It is obvious that what is affected by poetry of this character is our *will*, and not merely our intellectual powers pure and simple. The word *interest* means, therefore, that which arouses the concern of the individual will, *quod nostrâ interest ;* and here it is that beauty is clearly distinguished from interest. The one is an affair of the intellect, and that, too, of the purest and simplest kind. The other works upon the will. Beauty, then, consists in an apprehension of ideas; and knowledge of this character is beyond the range of the principle that nothing happens without a cause. Interest, on the other hand, has its origin nowhere but in the course of events; that is to say, in the complexities which are possible only through the action of this principle in its different forms.

We have now obtained a clear conception of the essential difference between the beauty and the interest of a work of art. We have recognised that beauty is the true end of every art, and therefore, also, of the poetic art. It now remains to raise the question whether the interest of a work of art is a second end, or a means to the exhibition of its beauty; or whether the interest of it is produced by its beauty as an essential concomitant, and comes of itself as soon as it is beautiful; or whether interest is at any rate compatible with the main end of art; or, finally, whether it is a hindrance to it.

In the first place, it is to be observed that the interest of a work of art is confined to works of poetic art. It does not exist in the case of fine art, or of music or architecture. Nay, with these forms of art it is not even conceivable, unless, indeed, the interest be of an entirely personal character, and confined to one or two spectators ; as, for example, where a picture is a portrait of some one whom we love or hate; the building, my house or my prison; the music, my wedding dance, or the tune to which I marched to the war. Interest of this kind is clearly quite foreign to the essence and purpose of art; it disturbs our judgment in so far as it makes the purely artistic attitude impossible. It may be, indeed, that to a smaller extent this is true of all interest.

Now, since the interest of a work of art lies in the fact that we have the same kind of sympathy with a poetic representation as with reality, it is obvious that the representation must deceive us for the moment; and this it can do only by its truth. But truth is an element in perfect art. A picture, a poem, should be as true as nature itself; but at the same time it should lay stress on whatever forms the unique character of its subject by drawing out all its essential manifestations, and by rejecting everything that is unessential and accidental. The picture or the poem will thus emphasise its *idea*, and give us that *ideal truth* which is superior to nature.

Truth, then, forms the point that is common both to interest and beauty in a work of art, as it is its truth which produces the illusion. The fact that the truth of which I speak is *ideal truth* might, indeed, be detrimental to the illusion, since it is just here that we have the general difference between poetry and reality, art and nature. But since it is possible for reality to coincide with the ideal, it is not actually necessary that this difference should destroy the illusion. In the case of the fine arts there is, in the range of the means which art adopts, a certain limit, and beyond it illusion is impossible. Sculpture, that

is to say, gives us mere colourless form; its figures are
without eyes and without movement; and painting
provides us with no more than a single view, enclosed
within strict limits, which separate the picture from
the adjacent reality. Here, then, there is no room for
illusion, and consequently none for that interest or
sympathy which resembles the interest we have in
reality; the will is at once excluded, and the object
alone is presented to us in a manner that frees it from
any personal concern.

It is a highly remarkable fact that a spurious kind
of fine art oversteps these limits, produces an illusion
of reality, and arouses our interest; but at the same
time it destroys the effect which fine art produces, and serves as nothing but a mere means
of exhibiting the beautiful, that is, of communicating
a knowledge of the ideas which it embodies. I refer
to *waxwork*. Here, we might say, is the dividing
line which separates it from the province of fine art.
When waxwork is properly executed, it produces a
perfect illusion; but for that very reason we approach
a wax figure as we approach a real man, who, as such,
is for the moment an object presented to our will.
That is to say, he is an object of interest; he
arouses the will, and consequently stills the intellect.
We come up to a wax figure with the same reserve
and caution as a real man would inspire in us: our
will is excited; it waits to see whether he is going to
be friendly to us, or the reverse, fly from us, or attack
us; in a word, it expects some action of him. But as
the figure, nevertheless, shows no sign of life, it produces the impression which is so very disagreeable.

namely, of a corpse. This is a case where the interest is of the most complete kind, and yet where there is no work of art at all. In other words, interest is not in itself a real end of art.

The same truth is illustrated by the fact that even in poetry it is only the dramatic and descriptive kind to which interest attaches; for if interest were, with beauty, the aim of art, poetry of the lyrical kind would, for that very reason, not take half so great a position as the other two.

In the second place, if interest were a means in the production of beauty, every interesting work would also be beautiful. That, however, is by no means the case. A drama or a novel may often attract us by its interest, and yet be so utterly deficient in any kind of beauty that we are afterwards ashamed of having wasted our time on it. This applies to many a drama which gives no true picture of the real life of man; which contains characters very superficially drawn, or so distorted as to be actual monstrosities, such as are not to be found in nature; but the course of events and the play of the action are so intricate, and we feel so much for the hero in the situation in which he is placed, that we are not content until we see the knot untangled and the hero rescued. The action is so cleverly governed and guided in its course that we remain in a state of constant curiosity as to what is going to happen, and we are utterly unable to form a guess; so that between eagerness and surprise our interest is kept active; and as we are pleasantly entertained, we do not notice the lapse of time. Most of Kotzebue's plays are of this character. For the mob this is the right thing : it looks for amusement, something to pass the time, not for intellectual perception. Beauty is an affair of such perception; hence sensibility to beauty varies as much as the intellectual faculties themselves. For the inner truth of a representation, and its correspondence with the real nature of humanity, the mob has no sense at all. What is flat and superficial it can grasp, but the depths of human nature are opened to it in vain.

It is also to be observed that dramatic representations which depend for their value on their interest lose by repetition, because they are no longer able to arouse curiosity as to their course, since it is already known. To see them often, makes them stale and tedious. On the other hand, works of which the value lies in their beauty gain by repetition, as they are then more and more understood.

Most novels are on the same footing as dramatic representations of this character. They are creatures of the same sort of imagination as we see in the story-teller of Venice and Naples, who lays a hat on the ground and waits until an audience is assembled. Then he spins a tale which so captivates his hearers that, when he gets to the catastrophe, he makes a round of the crowd, hat in hand, for contributions, without the least fear that his hearers will slip away. Similar story-tellers ply their trade in this country, though in a less direct fashion. They do it through the agency of publishers and circulating libraries. Thus they can avoid going about in rags, like their colleagues elsewhere; they can offer the children of their imagination to the public under the title of

novels, short stories, romantic poems, fairy tales, and
so on ; and the public, in a dressing-gown by the
fireside, sits down more at its ease, but also with a
greater amount of patience, to the enjoyment of the
interest which they provide.

How very little æsthetic value there generally is in
productions of this sort is well known ; and yet it
cannot be denied that many of them are interesting ;
or else how could they be so popular ?

We see, then, in reply to our second question, that
interest does not necessarily involve beauty ; and, con-
versely, it is true that beauty does not necessarily involve interest. Significant characters may be represented, that open up the depths of human nature, and
it may all be expressed in actions and sufferings of an
exceptional kind, so that the real nature of humanity
and the world may stand forth in the picture in the
clearest and most forcible lines ; and yet no high degree
of interest may be excited in the course of events
by the continued progress of the action, or by the
complexity and unexpected solution of the plot. The
immortal masterpieces of Shakespeare contain little
that excites interest ; the action does not go forward
in one straight line, but falters, as in *Hamlet*, all
through the play ; or else it spreads out in breadth,
as in *The Merchant of Venice*, whereas length is the
proper dimension of interest ; or the scenes hang
loosely together, as in *Henry IV.* Thus it is that
Shakespeare's dramas produce no appreciable effect on
the mob.

The dramatic requirements stated by Aristotle, and
more particularly the unity of action, have in view

the interest of the piece rather than its artistic
beauty. It may be said, generally, that these requirements are drawn up in accordance with the principle
of sufficient reason to which I have referred above.
We know, however, that the *idea*, and, consequently,
the beauty of a work of art, exist only for the perceptive intelligence which has freed itself from the
domination of that principle. It is just here that we
find the distinction between interest and beauty ; as
it is obvious that interest is part and parcel of the
mental attitude which is governed by the principle,
whereas beauty is always beyond its range. The
best and most striking refutation of the Aristotelian
unities is Manzoni's. It may be found in the preface to his dramas.

What is true of Shakespeare's dramatic works is
true also of Goethe's. Even *Egmont* makes little effect
on the public, because it contains scarcely any com-
plication or development : and if *Egmont* fails, what
are we to say of *Tasso* or *Iphigenia?* That the
Greek tragedians did not look to interest as a means
of working upon the public, is clear from the fact that
the material of their masterpieces was almost always
known to every one : they selected events which had
often been treated dramatically before. This shows
us how sensitive was the Greek public to the beautiful, as it did not require the interest of unexpected
events and new stories to season its enjoyment.

Neither does the quality of interest often attach to
masterpieces of descriptive poetry. Father Homer
lays the world and humanity before us in its true
nature, but he takes no trouble to attract our sym-

pathy by a complexity of circumstance, or to surprise us by unexpected entanglements. His pace is lingering; he stops at every scene; he puts one picture after another tranquilly before us, elaborating it with care. We experience no passionate emotion in reading him; our demeanour is one of pure perceptive intelligence; he does not arouse our will, but sings it to rest; and it costs us no effort to break off in our reading, for we are not in a condition of eager curiosity. This is all still more true of Dante, whose work is not, in the proper sense of the word, an epic, but a descriptive poem. The same thing may be said of the four immortal romances : *Don Quixote*, *Tristram Shandy*, *La Nouvelle Heloïse*, and *Wilhelm Meister*. To arouse our interest is by no means the chief aim of these works; in *Tristram Shandy* the hero, even at the end of the book, is only eight years of age.

On the other hand, we must not venture to assert that the quality of interest is not to be found in masterpieces of literature. We have it in Schiller's dramas in an appreciable degree, and consequently they are popular; also in the *Œdipus Rex* of Sophocles. Amongst masterpieces of description, we find it in Ariosto's *Orlando Furioso*; nay, an example of a high degree of interest, bound up with the beautiful, is afforded in an excellent novel by Walter Scott—*The Heart of Midlothian*. This is the most interesting work of fiction that I know, where all the effects due to interest, as I have given them generally in the preceding remarks, may be most clearly observed. At the same time it is a very beautiful romance throughout; it shows the most varied pictures of life, drawn with striking truth; and it exhibits highly different characters with great justice and fidelity.

Interest, then, is certainly compatible with beauty. That was our third question. Nevertheless, a comparatively small admixture of the element of interest may well be found to be most advantageous as far as beauty is concerned; for beauty is and remains the end of art. Beauty is in twofold opposition with interest; firstly, because it lies in the perception of the idea, and such perception takes its object entirely out of the range of the forms enunciated by the principle of sufficient reason; whereas interest has its sphere mainly in circumstance, and it is out of this principle that the complexity of circumstance arises. Secondly, interest works by exciting the will; whereas beauty exists only for the pure perceptive intelligence, which has no will. However, with dramatic and descriptive literature an admixture of interest is necessary, just as a volatile and gaseous substance requires a material basis if it is to be preserved and transferred. The admixture is necessary, partly, indeed, because interest is itself created by the events which have to be devised in order to set the characters in motion; partly because our minds would be weary of watching scene after scene if they had no concern for us, or of passing from one significant picture to another if we were not drawn on by some secret thread. It is this that we call interest: it is the sympathy which the event in itself forces us to feel, and which, by riveting our attention, makes the mind obedient to the poet, and able to follow him into all the parts of his story.

If the interest of a work of art is sufficient to achieve this result, it does all that can be required of it; for its only service is to connect the pictures by which the poet desires to communicate a knowledge of the idea, as if they were pearls, and interest were the thread that holds them together, and makes an ornament out of the whole.   But interest is prejudicial to beauty as soon as it oversteps this limit; and this is the case if we are so led away by the interest of a work that whenever we come to any detailed description in a novel, or any lengthy reflection on the part of a character in a drama, we grow impatient and want to put spurs to our author, so that we may follow the development of events with greater speed.   Epic and dramatic writings, where beauty and interest are both present in a high degree, may be compared to the working of a watch, where interest is the spring which keeps all the wheels in motion.   If it worked unhindered, the watch would run down in a few minutes.   Beauty, holding us in the spell of description and reflection, is like the barrel which checks its movement.

Or we may say that interest is the body of a poetic work, and beauty the soul.   In the epic and the drama, interest, as a necessary quality of the action, is the matter; and beauty, the form that requires the matter in order to be visible.

PSYCHOLOGICAL OBSERVATIONS.

PSYCHOLOGICAL OBSERVATIONS.

In the moment when a great affliction overtakes us, we are hurt to find that the world about us is unconcerned and goes its own way. As Goethe says in *Tasso*, how easily it leaves us helpless and alone, and continues its course like the sun and the moon and the other gods :—

> . . . *die Welt, wie sie so leicht,*
> *Uns hülflos, einsam lässt, und ihren Weg,*
> *Wie Sonn' und Mond und andre Götter geht.*

Nay more! it is something intolerable that even we ourselves have to go on with the mechanical round of our daily business, and that thousands of our own actions are and must be unaffected by the pain that throbs within us. And so, to restore the harmony between our outward doings and our inward feelings, we storm and shout, and tear our hair, and stamp with pain or rage.

Our temperament is so *despotic* that we are not satisfied unless we draw everything into our own life, and force all the world to sympathise with us. The only way of achieving this would be to win the love of others, so that the afflictions which oppress our own hearts might oppress theirs as well. Since that is attended with some difficulty, we often choose the shorter way, and blab out our burden of woe to people who do not care, and listen with curiosity, but without sympathy, and much oftener with satisfaction.

.   .   .   .

Speech and the communication of thought, which, in their mutual relations, are always attended by a slight impulse on the part of the will, are almost a physical necessity. Sometimes, however, the lower animals entertain me much more than the average man. For, in the first place, what can such a man say ? It is only conceptions, that is, the driest of ideas, that can be communicated by means of words; and what sort of conceptions has the average man to communicate, if he does not merely tell a story or give a report, neither of which makes conversation ? The greatest charm of conversation is the mimetic part of it,—the character that is manifested, be it never so little. Take the best of men : how little he can *say* of what goes on within him, since it is only conceptions that are communicable ; and yet a conversation with a clever man is one of the greatest of pleasures.

It is not only that ordinary men have little to say, but what intellect they have puts them in the way of concealing and distorting it ; and it is the necessity of practising this concealment that gives them such a pitiable character ; so that what they exhibit is not even the little that they have, but a mask and disguise. The lower animals, which have no reason, can conceal nothing ; they are altogether *naïve*, and therefore very entertaining, if we have only an eye for the kind of communications which they make. They speak not with words, but with shape and structure, and manner of life, and the things they set about; they express themselves, to an intelligent observer, in a very pleasing and entertaining fashion. It is a varied life that is presented to him, and one that in its manifestation is very different from his own; and yet essentially it is the same. He sees it in its simple form, when reflection is excluded; for with the lower animals life is lived wholly in and for the present moment: it is the present that the animal grasps; it has no care, or at least no conscious care, for the morrow, and no fear of death; and so it is wholly taken up with life and living.

· · · · · · · ·

The conversation among ordinary people, when it does not relate to any special matter of fact, but takes a more general character, mostly consists in hackneyed commonplaces, which they alternately repeat to each other with the utmost complacency.[1]

· · · · · · · ·

Some men can despise any blessing as soon as they cease to possess it; others only when they have obtained it. The latter are the more unhappy, and the nobler, of the two.

· · · · · · · ·

When the aching heart grieves no more over any particular object, but is oppressed by life as a whole, it withdraws, as it were, into itself. There is here a retreat and gradual extinction of the will, whereby the body, which is the manifestation of the will, is slowly but surely undermined; and the in-

---

[1] *Translator's Note.* This observation is in Schopenhauer's own English.

dividual experiences a steady dissolution of his bonds,
—a quiet presentiment of death. Hence the heart
which aches has a secret joy of its own; and it is this,
I fancy, which the English call " the joy of grief ".

The pain that extends to life as a whole, and
loosens our hold on it, is the only pain that is really
tragic. That which attaches to particular objects is
a will that is broken, but not resigned; it exhibits
the struggle and inner contradiction of the will and
of life itself; and it is comic, be it never so violent.
It is like the pain of the miser at the loss of his
hoard. Even though pain of the tragic kind proceeds
from a single definite object, it does not remain there;
it takes the separate affliction only as a *symbol* of life
as a whole, and transfers it thither.

.   .   .   .

Vexation is the attitude of the individual as intelligence towards the check imposed upon a strong
manifestation of the individual as will. There are
two ways of avoiding it: either by repressing the
violence of the will—in other words, by virtue; or by
keeping the intelligence from dwelling upon the
check—in other words, by Stoicism.

.   .   .   .

To win the favour of a very beautiful woman by
one's personality alone is perhaps a greater satisfaction to one's vanity than to anything else; for it is an
assurance that one's personality is an equivalent for
the person that is treasured and desired and deified
above all others. Hence it is that despised love is so
great a pang, especially when it is associated with
well-founded jealousy.

With this joy and this pain, it is probable that
vanity is more largely concerned than the senses,
because it is only the things of the mind, and not
mere sensuality, that produce such violent convul-
sions. The lower animals are familiar with lust, but
not with the passionate pleasures and pains of love.

   .   .   .   .

To be suddenly placed in a strange town or country
where the manner of life, possibly even the language,
is very different from our own, is, at the first moment,
like stepping into cold water. We are brought into
sudden contact with a new temperature, and we feel
a powerful and superior influence from without which
affects us uncomfortably. We find ourselves in a
strange element, where we cannot move with ease;
and, over and above that, we have the feeling that
while everything strikes us as strange, we ourselves
strike others in the same way. But as soon as we are
a little composed and reconciled to our surroundings,
as soon as we have appropriated some of its temperature, we feel an extraordinary sense of satisfaction, as
in bathing in cool water; we assimilate ourselves to
the new element, and cease to have any necessary pre-
occupation with our person. We devote our attention
undisturbed to our environment, to which we now feel
ourselves superior by being able to view it in an
objective and disinterested fashion, instead of being
oppressed by it, as before.

   .   .   .   .

When we are on a journey, and all kinds of
remarkable objects press themselves on our attention,
the intellectual food which we receive is often so

large in amount that we have no time for digestion;
and we regret that the impressions which succeed one
another so quickly leave no permanent trace.   But at
bottom it is the same with travelling as with reading.
How often do we complain that we cannot remember
one thousandth part of what we read!   In both cases,
however, we may console ourselves with the reflection
that the things we see and read make an impression
on the mind before they are forgotten, and so con-
tribute to its formation and nurture; while that
which we only remember does no more than stuff it
and puff it out, filling up its hollows with matter that
will always be strange to it, and leaving it in itself
a blank.

     .   .   .   .

It is the very many and varied forms in which
human life is presented to us on our travels that
make them entertaining.   But we never see more
than its outside, such as is everywhere open to public
view and accessible to strangers.   On the other hand,
human life on its inside, the heart and centre, where
it lives and moves and shows its character, and in
particular that part of the inner side which could be
seen at home amongst our relatives, is not seen; we
have exchanged it for the outer side.   This is why on
our travels we see the world like a painted landscape,
with a very wide horizon, but no foreground; and
why, in time, we get tired of it.

     .   .   .   .

One man is more concerned with the impression
which he makes upon the rest of mankind; another,
with the impression which the rest of mankind makes

upon him. The disposition of the one is subjective; of the other, objective; the one is, in the whole of his existence, more in the nature of an idea which is merely presented; the other, more of the being who presents it.

. . . .

A woman (with certain exceptions which need not be mentioned) will not take the first step with a man; for in spite of all the beauty she may have, she risks a refusal. A man may be ill in mind or body, or busy, or gloomy, and so not care for advances; and a refusal would be a blow to her vanity. But as soon as he takes the first step, and helps her over this danger, he stands on a footing of equality with her, and will generally find her quite tractable.

. . . .

The praise with which many men speak of their wives is really given to their own judgment in selecting them. This arises, perhaps, from a feeling of the truth of the saying, that a man shows what he is by the way in which he dies, and by the choice of his wife.

. . . .

If education or warning were of any avail, how could Seneca's pupil be a Nero?

. . . .

The Pythagorean[1] principle that *like is known only by like* is in many respects a true one. It explains how it is that every man understands his fellow only in so far as he resembles him, or, at least, is of a similar character. What one man is quite sure of per-

[1] See Porphyry, *de Vita Pythagorae.*

ceiving in another is that which is common to all, namely, the vulgar, petty or mean elements of our nature; here every man has a perfect understanding of his fellows; but the advantage which one man has over another does not exist for the other, who, be the talents in question as extraordinary as they may, will never see anything beyond what he possesses himself, for the very good reason that this is all he wants to see. If there is anything on which he is in doubt, it will give him a vague sense of fear, mixed with pique; because it passes his comprehension, and therefore is uncongenial to him.

This is why it is mind alone that understands mind; why works of genius are wholly understood and valued only by a man of genius, and why it must necessarily be a long time before they indirectly attract attention at the hands of the crowd, for whom they will never, in any true sense, exist. This, too, is why one man will look another in the face, with the impudent assurance that he will never see anything but a miserable resemblance of himself; and this is just what he will see, as he cannot grasp anything beyond it. Hence the bold way in which one man will contradict another. Finally, it is for the same reason that great superiority of mind isolates a man, and that those of high gifts keep themselves aloof from the vulgar (and that means every one); for if they mingle with the crowd, they can communicate only such parts of them as they share with the crowd, and so make themselves *common*. Nay, even though they possess some well-founded and authoritative reputation amongst the crowd, they are not long in losing it, together with any personal weight it may give them, since all are blind to the qualities on which it is based, but have their eyes open to anything that is vulgar and common to themselves. They soon discover the truth of the Arabian proverb: *Joke with a slave, and he'll show you his heels.*

It also follows that a man of high gifts, in his intercourse with others, must always reflect that the best part of him is out of sight in the clouds; so that if he desires to know accurately how much he can be to any one else, he has only to consider how much the man in question is to him. This, as a rule, is precious little; and therefore he is as uncongenial to the other, as the other to him.

. . . .

Goethe says somewhere that man is not without a vein of veneration. To satisfy this impulse to venerate, even in those who have no sense for what is really worthy, substitutes are provided in the shape of princes and princely families, nobles, titles, orders, and money-bags.

. . . .

Vague longing and boredom are close akin.

. . . .

When a man is dead, we envy him no more; and we only half envy him when he is old.

. . . .

Misanthropy and love of solitude are convertible ideas.

. . . .

In chess, the object of the game, namely, to checkmate one's opponent, is of arbitrary adoption; of the

6

possible means of attaining it, there is a great number; and according as we make a prudent use of them, we arrive at our goal. We enter on the game of our own choice.

Nor is it otherwise with human life, only that here the entrance is not of our choosing, but is forced on us; and the object, which is to live and exist, seems, indeed, at times as though it were of arbitrary adoption, and that we could, if necessary, relinquish it. Nevertheless it is, in the strict sense of the word, a natural object; that is to say, we cannot relinquish it without giving up existence itself. If we regard our existence as the work of some arbitrary power outside us, we must, indeed, admire the cunning by which that creative mind has succeeded in making us place so much value on an object which is only momentary and must of necessity be laid aside very soon, and which we see, moreover, on reflection, to be altogether vanity—in making, I say, this object so dear to us that we eagerly exert all our strength in working at it; although we know that as soon as the game is over, the object will exist for us no longer, and that, on the whole, we cannot say what it is that makes it so attractive. Nay, it seems to be an object as arbitrarily adopted as that of checkmating our opponent's king; and, nevertheless, we are always intent on the means of attaining it, and think and brood over nothing else. It is clear that the reason of it is that our intellect is only capable of looking outside, and has no power at all of looking within; and, since this is so, we have come to the conclusion that we must make the best of it.

ON THE WISDOM OF LIFE: APHORISMS.

ON THE WISDOM OF LIFE: APHORISMS.

THE simple Philistine believes that life is something infinite and unconditioned, and tries to look upon it and live it as though it left nothing to be desired. By method and principle the learned Philistine does the same: he believes that his methods and his principles are unconditionally perfect and objectively valid; so that as soon as he has found them, he has nothing to do but apply them to circumstances, and then approve or condemn. But happiness and truth are not to be seized in this fashion. It is phantoms of them alone that are sent to us here, to stir us to action; the average man pursues the shadow of happiness with unwearied labour; and the thinker, the shadow of truth; and both, though phantoms are all they have, possess in them as much as they can grasp. Life is a language in which certain truths are conveyed to us; could we learn them in some other way, we should not live. Thus it is that wise sayings and prudential maxims will never make up for the lack of experience, or be a substitute for life itself. Still they are not to be despised; for they, too, are a part of life; nay, they should be highly esteemed and regarded as the loose pages which others have copied from the book of truth as it is imparted by the spirit of the world. But they are pages which must needs be imperfect, and can never replace the real living voice. Still less can this be so when we reflect that life, or the book of truth, speaks differently to us all ; like the apostles who preached at Pentecost, and instructed the multitude, appearing to each man to speak in his own tongue.

.   .   .   .

Recognise the truth in yourself, recognise yourself in the truth ; and in the same moment you will find, to your astonishment, that the home which you have long been looking for in vain, which has filled your most ardent dreams, is there in its entirety, with every detail of it true, in the very place where you stand. It is there that your heaven touches your earth.

.   .   .   .

What makes us almost inevitably ridiculous is our serious way of treating the passing moment, as though it necessarily had all the importance which it seems to have. It is only a few great minds that are above this weakness, and, instead of being laughed at, have come to laugh themselves.

.   .   .   .

The bright and good moments of our life ought to teach us how to act aright when we are melancholy and dull and stupid, by preserving the memory of their results ; and the melancholy, dull, and stupid moments should teach us to be modest when we are bright. For we generally value ourselves according to our best and brightest moments ; and those in which we are weak and dull and miserable, we regard as no proper part of us. To remember them will teach us to be modest, humble, and tolerant.

Mark my words once for all, my dear friend, and be clever. Men are entirely self-centred, and incapable of looking at things objectively. If you had a dog and wanted to make him fond of you, and fancied that of your hundred rare and excellent characteristics the mongrel would be sure to perceive one, and that that would be sufficient to make him devoted to you body and soul—if, I say, you fancied that, you would be a fool. Pat him, give him something to eat; and for the rest, be what you please : he will not in the least care, but will be your faithful and devoted dog. Now, believe me, it is just the same with men—exactly the same. As Goethe says, man or dog, it is a miserable wretch :—

Denn ein erbärmlicher Schuft, so wie der Mensch, ist der Hund.

If you ask why these contemptible fellows are so lucky, it is just because, in themselves and for themselves and to themselves, they are nothing at all. The value which they possess is merely comparative ; they exist only for others ; they are never more than means ; they are never an end and object in themselves ; they are mere bait, set to catch others.[1] I do not admit that this rule is susceptible of any exceptions, that is to say, complete exceptions. There are, it is true, men—though they are sufficiently rare —who enjoy some subjective moments ; nay, there a' perhaps some who for every hundred subjectiv· moments enjoy a few that are objective ; but a higher state of perfection scarcely ever occurs. But do not

---

[1] All this is very euphemistically expressed in the Sophoclean verse :—

χάρις χάριν γὰρ ἐστιν ἡ τίκτουσ' ἀει.

take yourself for an exception : examine your love, your friendship, and consider if your objective judgments are not mostly subjective judgments in disguise ; consider if you duly recognise the good qualities of a man who is not fond of you.   Then be tolerant : confound it ! it's your duty.   As you are all so self-centred, recognise your own weakness.   You know that you cannot like a man who does not show himself friendly to you ; you know that he cannot do so for any length of time unless he likes you, and that he cannot like you unless you show that you are friendly to him ; then do it : your false friendliness will gradually become a true one.   Your own weakness and subjectivity must have some illusion.

This is really an *à priori* justification of politeness ; but I could give a still deeper reason for it.

.   .   .   .

Consider that chance, which, with error, its brother, and folly, its aunt, and malice, its grandmother, rules in this world ; which, every year and every day, by blows great and small, embitters the life of every son of earth, and yours too ; consider, I say, that it is to this wicked power that you owe your prosperity and independence ; for it gave you what it refused to many thousands, just to be able to give it to individuals like you.   Remembering all this, you will not behave as though you had a right to the possession of its gifts ; but you will perceive what a capricious mistress it is that gives you her favours ; and therefore when she takes it into her head to deprive you of some or all of them, you will not make a great fuss about her injustice ; but you will recognise that what chance gave, chance has taken away; if needs be, you will observe that this power is not quite so favourable to you as she seemed to be hitherto. Why, she might have disposed not only of what she gave you, but also of your honest and hard-earned gains.

But if chance still remains so favourable to you as to give you more than almost all others whose path in life you may care to examine, oh! be happy; do not struggle for the possession of her presents; employ them properly; look upon them as property held from a capricious lord: use them wisely and well.

.   .   .   .

The Aristotelian principle of keeping the mean in all things is ill suited to be the moral law for which it was intended; but it may easily be the best general rule of worldly wisdom, the best precept for a happy life. For life is so full of uncertainty; there are on all sides so many discomforts, burdens, sufferings, dangers, that a safe and happy voyage can be accomplished only by steering carefully through the rocks. As a rule, the fear of the ills we know drives us into the contrary ills; the pain of solitude, for example, drives us into society, and the first society that comes; the discomforts of society drive us into solitude; we exchange a forbidding demeanour for incautious confidence, and so on. It is ever the mark of folly to avoid one vice by rushing into its contrary:—

Stulti dum vitant vitia in contraria currunt.

Or else we think that we shall find satisfaction in something, and spend all our efforts on it; and thereby we omit to provide for the satisfaction of a hundred other wishes which make themselves felt at their own time. One loss and omission follows another, and there is no end to the misery.

Μηδὲν ἄγαν and *nil admirari* are, therefore, excellent rules of worldly wisdom.

.   .   .   .

We often find that people of great experience are the most frank and cordial in their intercourse with complete strangers, in whom they have no interest whatever. The reason of this is that men of experience know that it is almost impossible for people who stand in any sort of mutual relation to be sincere and open with one another; but that there is always more or less of a strain between them, due to the fact that they are looking after their own interests, whether immediate or remote. They regret the fact, but they know that it is so; hence they leave their own people, rush into the arms of a complete stranger, and in happy confidence open their hearts to him. Thus it is that monks and the like, who have given up the world and are strangers to it, are such good people to turn to for advice.

.   .   .   .

It is only by practising mutual restraint and self denial that we can act and talk with other people; and, therefore, if we have to converse at all, it can only be with a feeling of resignation. For if we seek society, it is because we want fresh impressions: these come from without, and are therefore foreign to ourselves. If a man fails to perceive this, and, when he seeks the society of others, is unwilling to practise resignation, and absolutely refuses to deny himself nay, demands that others, who are altogether different from himself, shall nevertheless be just what he wants them to be for the moment, according to the degree of education which he has reached, or according to his intellectual powers or his mood—the man, I say, who does this, is in contradiction with himself. For while he wants some one who shall be different from himself, and wants him just because he is different, for the sake of society and fresh influence, he nevertheless demands that this other individual shall precisely resemble the imaginary creature who accords with his mood, and have no thoughts but those which he has himself.

Women are very liable to subjectivity of this kind; but men are not free from it either.

I observed once to Goethe, in complaining of the illusion and vanity of life, that when a friend is with us we do not think the same of him as when he is away. He replied : " Yes! because the absent friend is yourself, and he exists only in your head ; whereas the friend who is present has an individuality of his own, and moves according to laws of his own, which cannot always be in accordance with those which you form for yourself ".

   .   .   .   .

A good supply of resignation is of the first importance in providing for the journey of life. It is a supply which we shall have to extract from disappointed hopes ; and the sooner we do it, the better for the rest of the journey.

   .   .   .   .

How should a man be content so long as he fails to

obtain complete unity in his inmost being? For as long as two voices alternately speak in him, what is right for one must be wrong for the other. Thus he is always complaining. But has any man ever been completely at one with himself? Nay, is not the very thought a contradiction?

That a man shall attain this inner unity is the impossible and inconsistent pretension put forward by almost all philosophers.[1] For as a man it is natural to him to be at war with himself as long as he lives. While he can be only one thing thoroughly, he has the disposition to be everything else, and the inalienable possibility of being it. If he has made his choice of one thing, all the other possibilities are always open to him, and are constantly claiming to be realised; and he has therefore to be continuously keeping them back, and to be overpowering and killing them as long as he wants to be that one thing. For example, if he wants to think only, and not to act and do business, the disposition to the latter is not thereby destroyed all at once; but as long as the thinker lives, he has every hour to keep on killing the acting and pushing man that is within him; always battling with himself, as though he were a monster whose head is no sooner struck off than it grows again. In the same way, if he is resolved to be a saint, he must kill himself so far as he is a being that enjoys and is given over to pleasure; for such he remains as long as he lives. It is not once for all that he must kill himself: he must keep on doing it all his life.

[1] *Audacter licet profitearis, summum bonum esse animi concordiam.* —Seneca.

If he has resolved upon pleasure, whatever be the way in which it is to be obtained, his lifelong struggle is with a being that desires to be pure and free and holy; for the disposition remains, and he has to kill it every hour. And so on in everything, with infinite modifications; it is now one side of him, and now the other, that conquers; he himself is the battlefield. If one side of him is continually conquering, the other is continually struggling; for its life is bound up with his own, and, as a man, he is the possibility of many contradictions.

How is inner unity even possible under such circumstances? It exists neither in the saint nor in the sinner; or rather, the truth is that no man is wholly one or the other. For it is *men* they have to be; that is, luckless beings, fighters and gladiators in the arena of life.

To be sure, the best thing he can do is to recognise which part of him smarts the most under defeat, and let it always gain the victory. This he will always be able to do by the use of his reason, which is an ever-present fund of ideas. Let him resolve of his own free will to undergo the pain which the defeat of the other part involves. This is *character*. For the battle of life cannot be waged free from all pain; it cannot come to an end without bloodshed; and in any case a man must suffer pain, for he is the conquered as well as the conqueror. *Haec est vivendi conditio.*

     .   .   .   .

The clever man, when he converses, will think less of what he is saying than of the person with whom he is speaking; for then he is sure to say nothing which he will afterwards regret; he is sure not to lay himself open, nor to commit an indiscretion. But his conversation will never be particularly interesting.

An intellectual man readily does the opposite, and with him the person with whom he converses is often no more than the mere occasion of a monologue; and it often happens that the other then makes up for his subordinate *rôle* by lying in wait for the man of intellect, and drawing his secrets out of him.

.   .   .   .

Nothing betrays less knowledge of humanity than to suppose that, if a man has a great many friends, it is a proof of merit and intrinsic value: as though men gave their friendship according to value and merit! as though they were not, rather, just like dogs, which love the person that pats them and gives them bits of meat, and never trouble themselves about anything else! The man who understands how to pat his fellows best, though they be the nastiest brutes,— that's the man who has many friends.

It is the converse that is true. Men of great intellectual worth, or, still more, men of genius, can have only very few friends; for their clear eye soon discovers all defects, and their sense of rectitude is always being outraged afresh by the extent and the horror of them. It is only extreme necessity that can compel such men not to betray their feelings, or even to stroke the defects as if they were beautiful additions. Personal love (for we are not speaking of the reverence which is gained by authority) cannot be won by a man of genius, unless the gods have endowed him with an indestructible cheerfulness of temper, a glance that makes the world look beautiful, or unless he has succeeded by degrees in taking men exactly as they are; that is to say, in making a fool of the fools, as is right and proper. On the heights we must expect to be solitary.

. . . .

Our constant discontent is for the most part rooted in the impulse of self-preservation. This passes into a kind of selfishness, and makes a duty out of the maxim that we should always fix our minds upon what we lack, so that we may endeavour to procure it. Thus it is that we are always intent on finding out what we want, and on thinking of it; but that maxim allows us to overlook undisturbed the things which we already possess; and so, as soon as we have obtained anything, we give it much less attention than before. We seldom think of what we have, but always of what we lack.

This maxim of egoism, which has, indeed, its advantages in procuring the means to the end in view, itself concurrently destroys the ultimate end, namely, contentment; like the bear in the fable that throws a stone at the hermit to kill the fly on his nose. We ought to wait until need and privation announce themselves, instead of looking for them. Minds that are naturally content do this, while hypochondrists do the reverse.

. . . .

A man's nature is in harmony with itself when he desires to be nothing but what he is; that is to say, when he has attained by experience a knowledge of his strength and of his weakness, and makes use of the one and conceals the other, instead of playing with false coin, and trying to show a strength which he does not possess. It is a harmony which produces an agreeable and rational character; and for the simple reason that everything which makes the man and gives him his mental and physical qualities is nothing but the manifestation of his will; is, in fact, what he *wills*. Therefore it is the greatest of all inconsistencies to wish to be other than we are.

.   .   .   .

People of a strange and curious temperament can be happy only under strange circumstances, such as suit their nature, in the same way as ordinary circumstances suit the ordinary man; and such circumstances can arise only if, in some extraordinary way, they happen to meet with strange people of a character different indeed, but still exactly suited to their own. That is why men of rare or strange qualities are seldom happy.

.   .   .   .

All pleasure is derived from the use and consciousness of power; and the greatest of pains that a man can feel is to perceive that his powers fail just when he wants to use them. Therefore it will be advantageous for every man to discover what powers he possesses, and what powers he lacks. Let him, then, develop the powers in which he is pre-eminent, and make a strong use of them; let him pursue the path where they will avail him; and even though he has to conquer his inclinations, let him avoid the path where such powers are requisite as he possesses only in a low degree. In this way he will often have a pleasant consciousness of strength, and seldom a painful consciousness of weakness; and it will go well with him.   But if he lets himself be drawn into efforts demanding a kind of strength quite different from that in which he is pre-eminent, he will experience humiliation; and this is perhaps the most painful feeling with which a man can be afflicted.

Yet there are two sides to everything.   The man who has insufficient self-confidence in a sphere where he has little power, and is never ready to make a venture, will on the one hand not even learn how to use the little power that he has; and on the other, in a sphere in which he would at least be able to achieve something, there will be a complete absence of effort, and consequently of pleasure.   This is always hard to bear; for a man can never draw a complete blank in any department of human welfare without feeling some pain.

.   .   .   .

As a child, one has no conception of the inexorable character of the laws of nature, and of the stubborn way in which everything persists in remaining what it is.   The child believes that even lifeless things are disposed to yield to it; perhaps because it feels itself one with nature, or, from mere unacquaintance with the world, believes that nature is disposed to be friendly.   Thus it was that when I was a child, and had thrown my shoe into a large vessel full of milk, I was discovered entreating the shoe to jump out. Nor is a child on its guard against animals until it learns that they are ill-natured and spiteful.   But not before we have gained mature experience do we

7

recognise that human character is unalterable; that no entreaty, or representation, or example, or benefit, will bring a man to give up his ways; but that, on the contrary, every man is compelled to follow his own mode of acting and thinking, with the necessity of a law of nature; and that, however we take him, he always remains the same. It is only after we have obtained a clear and profound knowledge of this fact that we give up trying to persuade people, or to alter them and bring them round to our way of thinking. We try to accommodate ourselves to theirs instead, so far as they are indispensable to us, and to keep away from them so far as we cannot possibly agree.

Ultimately we come to perceive that even in matters of mere intellect—although its laws are the same for all, and the subject as opposed to the object of thought does not really enter into individuality—there is, nevertheless, no certainty that the whole truth of any matter can be communicated to any one, or that any one can be persuaded or compelled to assent to it; because, as Bacon says, *intellectus humanus luminis sicci non est:* the light of the human intellect is coloured by interest and passion.

．　．　．　．　．　．　．　．　．

It is just because *all happiness is of a negative character* that, when we succeed in being perfectly at our ease, we are not properly conscious of it. Everything seems to pass us softly and gently, and hardly to touch us until the moment is over; and then it is the positive feeling of something lacking that tells us of the happiness which has vanished; it is then that we observe that we have failed to hold it fast, and we suffer the pangs of self-reproach as well as of privation.

   .   .   .   .

Every happiness that a man enjoys, and almost every friendship that he cherishes, rest upon illusion; for, as a rule, with increase of knowledge they are bound to vanish. Nevertheless, here as elsewhere, a man should courageously pursue truth, and never weary of striving to settle accounts with himself and the world. No matter what happens to the right or to the left of him,—be it a chimæra or fancy that makes him happy, let him take heart and go on, with no fear of the desert which widens to his view. Of one thing only must he be quite certain: that under no circumstances will he discover any lack of worth in himself when the veil is raised; the sight of it would be the Gorgon that would kill him. Therefore, if he wants to remain undeceived, let him in his inmost being feel his own worth. For to feel the lack of it is not merely the greatest, but also the only true affliction; all other sufferings of the mind may not only be healed, but may be immediately relieved, by the secure consciousness of worth. The man who is assured of it can sit down quietly under sufferings that would otherwise bring him to despair; and though he has no pleasures, no joys and no friends, he can rest in and on himself; so powerful is the comfort to be derived from a vivid consciousness of this advantage; a comfort to be preferred to every other earthly blessing. Contrarily, nothing in the world can relieve a man who knows his own worthlessness; all that he can do is to conceal it by deceiving people or deafening them with his noise; but neither expedient will serve him very long.

. . . .

We must always try to preserve large views. If we are arrested by details we shall get confused, and see things awry. The success or the failure of the moment, and the impression that they make, should count for nothing.[1]

. . . .

How difficult it is to learn to understand oneself, and clearly to recognise what it is that one wants before anything else; what it is, therefore, that is most immediately necessary to our happiness; then what comes next; and what takes the third and the fourth place, and so on.

Yet, without this knowledge, our life is planless, like a captain without a compass.

. . . .

The sublime melancholy which leads us to cherish a lively conviction of the worthlessness of everything, of all pleasures and of all mankind, and therefore to long for nothing, but to feel that life is merely a burden which must be borne to an end that cannot be very distant, is a much happier state of mind than any condition of desire, which, be it never so cheerful, would have us place a value on the illusions of the world, and strive to attain them.

This is a fact which we learn from experience; and it is clear, *à priori*, that one of these is a condition of illusion, and the other of knowledge.

---

[1] *Translator's Note.* Schopenhauer, for some reason that is not apparent, wrote this remark in French.

Whether it is better to marry or not to marry is a question which in very many cases amounts to this: Are the cares of love more endurable than the anxieties of a livelihood?

.　　.　　.　　.　　.　　.　　.

Marriage is a trap which nature sets for us.[1]

.　　.　　.　　.　　.　　.　　.

Poets and philosophers who are married men incur by that very fact the suspicion that they are looking to their own welfare, and not to the interests of science and art.

.　　.　　.　　.　　.　　.　　.

Habit is everything. Hence to be calm and unruffled is merely to anticipate a habit; and it is a great advantage not to need to form it.

.　　.　　.　　.　　.　　.　　.

"Personality is the element of the greatest happiness." Since *pain* and *boredom* are the two chief enemies of human happiness, nature has provided our personality with a protection against both. We can ward off pain, which is more often of the mind than of the body, by *cheerfulness*; and boredom by *intelligence*. But neither of these is akin to the other; nay, in any high degree they are perhaps incompatible. As Aristotle remarks, genius is allied to melancholy; and people of very cheerful disposition are only intelligent on the surface. The better, therefore, anyone is by nature armed against one of these evils, the worse, as a rule, is he armed against the other.

[1] *Translator's Note.* Also in French.

There is no human life that is free from pain and boredom; and it is a special favour on the part of fate if a man is chiefly exposed to the evil against which nature has armed him the better; if fate, that is, sends a great deal of pain where there is a very cheerful temper in which to bear it, and much leisure where there is much intelligence, but not *vice versâ*. For if a man is intelligent, he feels pain doubly or trebly; and a cheerful but unintellectual temper finds solitude and unoccupied leisure altogether unendurable.

.   .   .   .

In the sphere of thought, absurdity and perversity remain the masters of this world, and their dominion is suspended only for brief periods. Nor is it otherwise in art; for there genuine work, seldom found and still more seldom appreciated, is again and again driven out by dulness, insipidity, and affectation.

It is just the same in the sphere of action. Most men, says Bias, are bad. Virtue is a stranger in this world; and boundless egoism, cunning and malice, are always the order of the day. It is wrong to deceive the young on this point, for it will only make them feel later on that their teachers were the first to deceive them. If the object is to render the pupil a better man by telling him that others are excellent, it fails; and it would be more to the purpose to say Most men are bad, it is for you to be better. In this way he would, at least, be sent out into the world armed with a shrewd foresight, instead of having to be convinced by bitter experience that his teachers were wrong.

All ignorance is dangerous, and most errors must be dearly paid. And good luck must he have that carries unchastised an error in his head unto his death.[1]

.   .   .   .

Every piece of success has a doubly beneficial effect upon us when, apart from the special and material advantage which it brings, it is accompanied by the enlivening assurance that the world, fate, or the dæmon within, does not mean so badly with us, nor is so opposed to our prosperity as we had fancied; when, in fine, it restores our courage to live.

Similarly, every misfortune or defeat has, in the contrary sense, an effect that is doubly depressing.

.   .   .   .

If we were not all of us exaggeratedly interested in ourselves, life would be so uninteresting that no one could endure it.

.   .   .   .

Everywhere in the world, and under all circumstances, it is only by force that anything can be done; but power is mostly in bad hands, because baseness is everywhere in a fearful majority.

.   .   .   .

Why should it be folly to be always intent on getting the greatest possible enjoyment out of the moment, which is our only sure possession? Our whole life is no more than a magnified present, and in itself as fleeting.

.   .   .   .

As a consequence of his individuality and the posi-

[1] *Translator's Note.* This, again, is Schopenhauer's own English

tion in which he is placed, everyone without exception
lives in a certain state of limitation, both as regards
his ideas and the opinions which he forms. Another
man is also limited, though not in the same way;
but should he succeed in comprehending the other's
limitation he can confuse and abash him, and put him
to shame, by making him feel what his limitation is,
even though the other be far and away his superior.
Shrewd people often employ this circumstance to
obtain a false and momentary advantage.

.   .   .   .

The only genuine superiority is that of the mind
and character; all other kinds are fictitious, affected,
false; and it is good to make them feel that it is so
when they try to show off before the superiority that
is true.[1]

.   .   .   .

All the world's a stage,
And all the men and women merely players.

Exactly! Independently of what a man really is in
himself, he has a part to play, which fate has imposed
upon him from without, by determining his rank,
education, and circumstances. The most immediate
application of this truth appears to me to be that in
life, as on the stage, we must distinguish between the
actor and his part; distinguish, that is, the man in
himself from his position and reputation—from the
part which rank and circumstances have imposed upon
him. How often it is that the worst actor plays the
king, and the best the beggar! This may happen in

[1] *Translator's Note.* In the original this also is in French.

life, too; and a man must be very *crude* to confuse
the actor with his part.

.   .   .   .

Our life is so poor that none of the treasures of the
world can make it rich; for the sources of enjoyment
are soon found to be all very scanty, and it is in vain
that we look for one that will always flow.   Therefore,
as regards our own welfare, there are only two ways
in which we can use wealth.   We can either spend it
in ostentatious pomp, and feed on the cheap respect
which our imaginary glory will bring us from the
infatuated crowd; or, by avoiding all expenditure
that will do us no good, we can let our wealth
grow, so that we may have a bulwark against misfortune and want that shall be stronger and better
every day; in view of the fact that life, though it has
few delights, is rich in evils.

.   .   .   .

It is just because our real and inmost being is *will*
that it is only by its exercise that we can attain a vivid
consciousness of existence, although this is almost
always attended by pain.   Hence it is that existence
is essentially painful, and that many persons for whose
wants full provision is made arrange their day in
accordance with extremely regular, monotonous, and
definite habits.   By this means they avoid all the
pain which the movement of the will produces; but,
on the other hand, their whole existence becomes a
series of scenes and pictures that mean nothing.   They
are hardly aware that they exist.   Nevertheless, it is
the best way of settling accounts with life, so long as
there is sufficient change to prevent an excessive feel-

ing of boredom. It is much better still if the Muses
give a man some worthy occupation, so that the
pictures which fill his consciousness have some meaning, and yet not a meaning that can be brought into
any relation with his will.

.   .   .   .

A man is *wise* only on condition of living in a
world full of fools.

GENIUS AND VIRTUE.

GENIUS AND VIRTUE.

WHEN I think, it is the spirit of the world which is striving to express its thought; it is nature which is trying to know and fathom itself. It is not the thoughts of some other mind, which I am endeavouring to trace; but it is I who transform that which exists into something which is known and thought, and would otherwise neither come into being nor continue in it.

In the realm of physics it was held for thousands of years to be a fact beyond question that water was a simple and consequently an original element. In the same way in the realm of metaphysics it was held for a still longer period that the *ego* was a simple and consequently an indestructible entity. I have shown, however, that it is composed of two heterogeneous parts, namely, the *Will*, which is metaphysical in its character, a thing in itself, and the *knowing subject*, which is physical and a mere phenomenon.

Let me illustrate what I mean. Take any large, massive, heavy building: this hard, ponderous body that fills so much space exists, I tell you, only in the soft pulp of the brain. There alone, in the human brain, has it any being. Unless you understand this, you can go no further.

Truly it is the world itself that is a miracle; the

world of material bodies. I looked at two of them.
Both were heavy, symmetrical, and beautiful. One
was a jasper vase with golden rim and golden handles;
the other was an organism, an animal, a man. When
I had sufficiently admired their exterior, I asked my
attendant genius to allow me to examine the inside
of them; and I did so. In the vase I found nothing
but the force of gravity and a certain obscure desire,
which took the form of chemical affinity. But when
I entered into the other—how shall I express my
astonishment at what I saw? It is more incredible
than all the fairy tales and fables that were ever
conceived. Nevertheless, I shall try to describe it,
even at the risk of finding no credence for my tale.

In this second thing, or rather in the upper end of
it, called the head, which on its exterior side looks like
anything else—a body in space, heavy, and so on—
I found no less an object than the whole world itself,
together with the whole of the space in which all of it
exists, and the whole of the time in which all of it
moves, and finally everything that fills both time and
space in all its variegated and infinite character; nay,
strangest sight of all, I found myself walking about
in it! It was no picture that I saw; it was no
peep-show, but reality itself. This it is that is really
and truly to be found in a thing which is no bigger
than a cabbage, and which, on occasion, an executioner
might strike off at a blow, and suddenly smother that
world in darkness and night. The world, I say,
would vanish, did not heads grow like mushrooms,
and were there not always plenty of them ready to
snatch it up as it is sinking down into nothing, and

keep it going like a ball. This world is an idea which they all have in common, and they express the community of their thought by the word "objectivity".

In the face of this vision I felt as if I were Ardschuna when Krishna appeared to him in his true majesty, with his hundred thousand arms and eyes and mouths.

When I see a wide landscape, and realise that it arises by the operation of the functions of my brain, that is to say, of time, space, and causality, on certain spots which have gathered on my retina, I feel that I carry it within me. I have an extraordinarily clear consciousness of the identity of my own being with that of the external world.

Nothing provides so vivid an illustration of this identity as a *dream*. For in a dream other people appear to be totally distinct from us, and to possess the most perfect objectivity, and a nature which is quite different from ours, and which often puzzles, surprises, astonishes, or terrifies us; and yet it is all our own self. It is even so with the will, which sustains the whole of the external world and gives it life; it is the same will that is in ourselves, and it is there alone that we are immediately conscious of it. But it is the intellect, in ourselves and in others, which makes all these miracles possible; for it is the intellect which everywhere divides actual being into subject and object; it is a hall of phantasmagorical mystery, inexpressibly marvellous, incomparably magical.

The difference in degree of mental power which sets so wide a gulf between the genius and the ordinary mortal rests, it is true, upon nothing else than a more or less perfect development of the cerebral system.

But it is this very difference which is so important, because the whole of the real world in which we live and move possesses an existence only in relation to this cerebral system. Accordingly, the difference between a genius and an ordinary man is a total diversity of world and existence. The difference between man and the lower animals may be similarly explained.

When Momus was said to ask for a window in the breast, it was an allegorical joke, and we cannot even imagine such a contrivance to be a possibility; but it would be quite possible to imagine that the skull and its integuments were transparent, and then, good heavens! what differences should we see in the size, the form, the quality, the movement of the brain! what degrees of value! A great mind would inspire as much respect at first sight as three stars on a man's breast, and what a miserable figure would be cut by many a one who wore them!

Men of genius and intellect, and all those whose mental and theoretical qualities are far more developed than their moral and practical qualities—men, in a word, who have more mind than character—are often not only awkward and ridiculous in matters of daily life, as has been observed by Plato in the seventh book of the *Republic*, and portrayed by Goethe in his *Tasso;* but they are often, from a moral point of view, weak and contemptible creatures as well ; nay, they might almost be called bad men. Of this Rousseau has given us genuine examples. Nevertheless, that better consciousness which is the source of all virtue is often stronger in them than in many of

those whose actions are nobler than their thoughts;
nay, it may be said that those who think nobly have
a better acquaintance with virtue, while the others
make a better practice of it. Full of zeal for the
good and for the beautiful, they would fain fly up to
heaven in a straight line; but the grosser elements of
this earth oppose their flight, and they sink back
again. They are like born artists, who have no
knowledge of technique, or find that the marble is too
hard for their fingers. Many a man who has much
less enthusiasm for the good, and a far shallower
acquaintance with its depths, makes a better thing of
it in practice; he looks down upon the noble thinkers
with contempt, and he has a right to do it; nevertheless, he does not understand them, and they despise
him in their turn, and not unjustly. They are to blame;
for every living man has, by the fact of his living,
signed the conditions of life; but they are still more
to be pitied. They achieve their redemption, not on
the way of virtue, but on a path of their own; and
they are saved, not by works, but by faith.

Men of no genius whatever cannot bear solitude:
they take no pleasure in the contemplation of nature
and the world. This arises from the fact that they never
lose sight of their own will, and therefore they see
nothing of the objects of the world but the bearing of
such objects upon their will and person. With objects
which have no such bearing there sounds within them
a constant note: *It is nothing to me*, which is the
fundamental base in all their music. Thus all things
seem to them to wear a bleak, gloomy, strange, hostile
aspect. It is only for their will that they seem to have

8

any perceptive faculties at all; and it is, in fact, only a moral and not a theoretical tendency, only a moral and not an intellectual value, that their life possesses. The lower animals bend their heads to the ground, because all that they want to see is what touches their welfare, and they can never come to contemplate things from a really objective point of view. It is very seldom that unintellectual men make a true use of their erect position, and then it is only when they are moved by some intellectual influence outside them.

The man of intellect or genius, on the other hand, has more of the character of the eternal subject that knows, than of the finite subject that wills; his knowledge is not quite engrossed and captivated by his will, but passes beyond it; he is the son, *not of the bondwoman, but of the free.* It is not only a moral but also a theoretical tendency that is evinced in his life; nay, it might perhaps be said that to a certain extent he is beyond morality. Of great villainy he is totally incapable; and his conscience is less oppressed by ordinary sin than the conscience of the ordinary man, because life, as it were, is a game, and he sees through it.

The relation between *genius* and *virtue* is determined by the following considerations. Vice is an impulse of the will so violent in its demands that it affirms its own life by denying the life of others. The only kind of knowledge that is useful to the will is the knowledge that a given effect is produced by a certain cause. Genius itself is a kind of knowledge, namely, of ideas; and it is a knowledge which is unconcerned with any principle of causation. The man who is devoted to knowledge of this character is not employed in the business of the will. Nay, every man who is devoted to the purely objective contemplation of the world (and it is this that is meant by the knowledge of ideas) completely loses sight of his will and its objects, and pays no further regard to the interests of his own person, but becomes a pure intelligence free of any admixture of will.

Where, then, devotion to the intellect predominates over concern for the will and its objects, it shows that the man's will is not the principal element in his being, but that in proportion to his intelligence it is weak. Violent desire, which is the root of all vice, never allows a man to arrive at the pure and disinterested contemplation of the world, free from any relation to the will, such as constitutes the quality of genius; but here the intelligence remains the constant slave of the will.

Since genius consists in the perception of ideas, and men of genius *contemplate* their object, it may be said that it is only the eye which is any real evidence of genius. For the contemplative gaze has something steady and vivid about it; and with the eye of genius it is often the case, as with Goethe, that the white membrane over the pupil is visible. With violent, passionate men the same thing may also happen, but it arises from a different cause, and may be easily distinguished by the fact that the eyes roll. Men of no genius at all have no interest in the idea expressed by an object, but only in the relations in which that object stands to others, and finally to their

own person. Thus it is that they never indulge in
contemplation, or are soon done with it, and rarely
fix their eyes long upon any object; and so their eyes
do not wear the mark of genius which I have described. Nay, the regular Philistine does the direct
opposite of contemplating—he spies. If he looks at
anything it is to pry into it; as may be specially observed when he screws up his eyes, which he frequently
does, in order to see the clearer. Certainly, no real
man of genius ever does this, at least habitually, even
though he is short-sighted.

What I have said will sufficiently illustrate the
conflict between genius and vice. It may be, however, nay, it is often the case, that genius is attended
by a strong will; and as little as men of genius were
ever consummate rascals, were they ever perhaps
perfect saints either.

Let me explain. Virtue is not exactly a positive
weakness of the will; it is, rather, an intentional
restraint imposed upon its violence through a knowledge of it in its inmost being as manifested in the
world. This knowledge of the world, the inmost
being of which is communicable only in *ideas*, is
common both to the genius and to the saint. The
distinction between the two is that the genius reveals
his knowledge by rendering it in some form of his
own choice, and the product is Art. For this the
saint, as such, possesses no direct faculty; he makes
an immediate application of his knowledge to his own
will, which is thus led into a denial of the world.
With the saint knowledge is only a means to an end,
whereas the genius remains at the stage of know-

ledge, and has his pleasure in it, and reveals it by rendering what he knows in his art.

In the hierarchy of physical organisation, strength of will is attended by a corresponding growth in the intelligent faculties. A high degree of knowledge, such as exists in the genius, presupposes a powerful will, though, at the same time, a will that is subordinate to the intellect. In other words, both the intellect and the will are strong, but the intellect is the stronger of the two. Unless, as happens in the case of the saint, the intellect is at once applied to the will, or, as in the case of the artist, it finds its pleasures in a reproduction of itself, the will remains untamed. Any strength that it may lose is due to the predominance of the pure objective intelligence which is concerned with the contemplation of ideas, and is not, as in the case of the common or the bad man, wholly occupied with the objects of the will. In the interval, when the genius is no longer engaged in the contemplation of ideas, and his intelligence is again applied to the will and its objects, the will is re-awakened in all its strength. Thus it is that men of genius often have very violent desires, and are addicted to sensual pleasure and to anger. Great crimes, however, they do not commit; because, when the opportunity of them offers, they recognise their idea, and see it very vividly and clearly. Their intelligence is thus directed to the idea, and so gains the predominance over the will, and turns its course, as with the saint; and the crime is uncommitted.

The genius, then, always participates to some degree in the characteristic of the saint, as he is a

man of the same qualification; and, contrarily, the
saint always participates to some degree in the characteristics of the genius.

The good-natured character, which is common, is to
be distinguished from the saintly by the fact that it
consists in a weakness of will, with a somewhat less
marked weakness of intellect. A lower degree of the
knowledge of the world as revealed in ideas here
suffices to check and control a will that is weak in
itself. Genius and sanctity are far removed from
good-nature, which is essentially weak in all its manifestations.

Apart from all that I have said, so much at least is
clear. What appears under the forms of time, space,
and causality, and vanishes again, and in reality is
nothing, and reveals its nothingness by death—this
vicious and fatal appearance is the will. But what
does not appear, and is no phenomenon, but rather
the noumenon; what makes appearance possible;
what is not subject to the principle of causation, and
therefore has no vain or vanishing existence, but
abides for ever unchanged in the midst of a world
full of suffering, like a ray of light in a storm,—free,
therefore, from all pain and fatality,—this, I say, is
the intelligence. The man who is more intelligence
than will, is thereby delivered, in respect of the
greatest part of him, from nothingness and death;
and such a man is in his nature a genius.

By the very fact that he lives and works, the man
who is endowed with genius makes an entire sacrifice
of himself in the interests of everyone. Accordingly,
he is free from the obligation to make a particular

sacrifice for individuals ; and thus he can refuse many demands which others are rightly required to meet. He suffers and achieves more than all the others.

The spring which moves the genius to elaborate his works is not fame, for that is too uncertain a quality, and when it is seen at close quarters, of little worth. No amount of fame will make up for the labour of attaining it :—

Nulla est fama tuum par æquiparare laborem.

Nor is it the delight that a man has in his work ; for that too is outweighed by the effort which he has to make. It is, rather, an instinct *sui generis ;* in virtue of which the genius is driven to express what he sees and feels in some permanent shape, without being conscious of any further motive.

It is manifest that in so far as it leads an individual to sacrifice himself for his species, and to live more in the species than in himself, this impulse is possessed of a certain resemblance with such modifications of the sexual impulse as are peculiar to man. The modifications to which I refer are those that confine this impulse to certain individuals of the other sex, whereby the interests of the species are attained. The individuals who are actively affected by this impulse may be said to sacrifice themselves for the species, by their passion for each other, and the disadvantageous conditions thereby imposed upon them,—in a word, by the institution of marriage. They may be said to be serving the interests of the species, rather than the interests of the individual.

The instinct of the genius does, in a higher fashion,

for the idea, what passionate love does for the will.
In both cases there are peculiar pleasures and peculiar
pains reserved for the individuals who in this way
serve the interests of the species; and they live in a
state of enhanced power.

The genius who decides once for all to live for the
interests of the species in the way which he chooses
is neither fitted nor called upon to do it in the other.
It is a curious fact that the perpetuation of a man's
name is effected in both ways.

In music the finest compositions are the most
difficult to understand. They are only for the trained
intelligence. They consist of long movements, where
it is only after a labyrinthine maze that the fundamental note is recovered. It is just so with genius; it
is only after a course of struggle, and doubt, and error,
and much reflection and vacillation, that great minds
attain their equilibrium. It is the longest pendulum
that makes the greatest swing. Little minds soon
come to terms with themselves and the world, and
then fossilise; but the others flourish, and are always
alive and in motion.

The essence of genius is a measure of intellectual
power far beyond that which is required to serve the
individual's will. But it is a measure of a merely
relative character, and it may be reached by lowering
the degree of the will, as well as by raising that of
the intellect. There are men whose intellect predominates over their will, and are yet not possessed of
genius in any proper sense. Their intellectual powers
do, indeed, exceed the ordinary, though not to any
great extent, but their will is weak. They have no

violent desires; and therefore they are more concerned with mere knowledge than with the satisfaction of any aims. Such men possess talent; they are intelligent, and at the same time very contented and cheerful.

A clear, cheerful and reasonable mind, such as brings a man happiness, is dependent on the relation established between his intellect and his will—a relation in which the intellect is predominant. But genius and a great mind depend on the relation between a man's intellect and that of other people—a relation in which his intellect must exceed theirs, and at the same time his will may also be proportionately stronger. That is the reason why genius and happiness need not necessarily exist together.

When the individual is distraught by cares or pleasantry, or tortured by the violence of his wishes and desires, the genius in him is enchained and cannot move. It is only when care and desire are silent that the air is free enough for genius to live in it. It is then that the bonds of matter are cast aside, and the pure spirit—the pure, knowing subject—remains. Hence, if a man has any genius, let him guard himself from pain, keep care at a distance, and limit his desires; but those of them which he cannot suppress let him satisfy to the full. This is the only way in which he will make the best use of his rare existence, to his own pleasure and the world's profit.

To fight with need and care or desires, the satisfaction of which is refused and forbidden, is good enough work for those who, were they free of them, would have to fight with boredom, and so take to bad practices;

but not for the man whose time, if well used, will bear fruit for centuries to come. As Diderot says, he is not merely a moral being.

Mechanical laws do not apply in the sphere of chemistry, nor do chemical laws in the sphere in which organic life is kindled. In the same way, the rules which avail for ordinary men will not do for the exceptions, nor will their pleasures either.

It is a persistent, uninterrupted activity that constitutes the superior mind. The object to which this activity is directed is a matter of subordinate importance; it has no essential bearing on the superiority in question, but only on the individual who possesses it. All that education can do is to determine the direction which this activity shall take; and that is the reason why a man's nature is so much more important than his education. For education is to natural faculty what a wax nose is to a real one; or what the moon and the planets are to the sun. In virtue of his education a man says, not what he thinks himself, but what others have thought and he has learned as a matter of training; and what he does is not what he wants, but what he has been accustomed, to do.

The lower animals perform many intelligent functions much better than man; for instance, the finding of their way back to the place from which they came, the recognition of individuals, and so on. In the same way, there are many occasions in real life to which the genius is incomparably less equal and fitted than the ordinary man. Nay more: just as animals never commit a folly in the strict sense of the word, so the average man is not exposed to folly in the same degree as the genius.

The average man is wholly relegated to the sphere of *being*; the genius, on the other hand, lives and moves chiefly in the sphere of *knowledge*. This gives rise to a twofold distinction. In the first place, a man can be one thing only, but he may *know* countless things, and thereby, to some extent, identify himself with them, by participating in what Spinoza calls their *esse objectivum*. In the second place, the world, as I have elsewhere observed, is fine enough in appearance, but in reality dreadful; for torment is the condition of all life.

It follows from the first of these distinctions that the life of the average man is essentially one of the greatest boredom; and thus we see the rich warring against boredom with as much effort and as little respite as fall to the poor in their struggle with need and adversity. And from the second of them it follows that the life of the average man is overspread with a dull, turbid, uniform gravity; whilst the brow of genius glows with mirth of a unique character, which, although he has sorrows of his own more poignant than those of the average man, nevertheless breaks out afresh, like the sun through clouds. It is when the genius is overtaken by an affliction which affects others as well as himself, that this quality in him is most in evidence; for then he is seen to be like man, who alone can laugh, in comparison with the beast of the field, which lives out its life grave and dull.

It is the curse of the genius that in the same

measure in which others think him great and worthy of admiration, he thinks them small and miserable creatures. His whole life long he has to suppress this opinion; and, as a rule, they suppress theirs as well. Meanwhile, he is condemned to live in a bleak world, where he meets no equal, as it were an island where there are no inhabitants but monkeys and parrots. Moreover, he is always troubled by the illusion that from a distance a monkey looks like a man.

Vulgar people take a huge delight in the faults and follies of great men; and great men are equally annoyed at being thus reminded of their kinship with them.

The real dignity of a man of genius or great intellect, the trait which raises him over others and makes him worthy of respect, is at bottom the fact, that the only unsullied and innocent part of human nature, namely, the intellect, has the upper hand in him, and prevails; whereas, in the other there is nothing but sinful will, and just as much intellect as is requisite for guiding his steps,—rarely any more, very often somewhat less,—and of what use is it?

It seems to me that genius might have its root in a certain perfection and vividness of the memory as it stretches back over the events of past life. For it is only by dint of memory, which makes our life in the strict sense a complete whole, that we attain a more profound and comprehensive understanding of it.

THE END.

SCHOPENHAUER SERIES.

Uniformly Bound in Cloth.   Price 3s. 6d.

THE WISDOM OF LIFE.   Being the First Part of ARTHUR SCHOPENHAUER's *Aphorismen zur Lebensweisheit.*   Translated, with a Preface, by T. BAILEY SAUNDERS, M.A. *Twelfth Edition.*

PRESS NOTICES.

" Schopenhauer is not simply a moralist writing in his study and applying abstract principles to the conduct of thought and action, but is also in a large measure a man of the world, with a firm grasp of the actual, and is therefore able to speak in a way which, to use Bacon's phrase, comes home to men's business and bosoms. The essentially practical character of his ' Wisdom of Life ' is evidenced by his frequent recourse to illustrations, and his singularly apt use of them. . . . This allusive, illustrative method of treatment gives to his work a special charm in which similar treatises are, as a rule, deficient.   Mr. Bailey Saunders' introductory essay adds much to the value and interest of a singularly suggestive volume." —*Manchester Examiner.*

" Schopenhauer, as seen through the medium of Mr. Saunders' translation, might easily become a widely-read and popular preacher among us. . . . We are very much indebted to Mr. Saunders for his neat little essay as an introduction to an author interesting and easily understanded of the people." — *Cambridge Review.*

"From the point of view of the English reader there is a good deal to be said in favour of taking Schopenhauer in small doses, commencing with the less technical of the philosopher's writings, such as treat of subjects interesting to the human kind—a course made easy by Mr. Bailey Saunders' fluent translations."—*Saturday Review.*

———————

COUNSELS AND MAXIMS: Being the Second Part of ARTHUR SCHOPENHAUER'S *Aphorismen zur Lebensweisheit.* Translated by T. BAILEY SAUNDERS, M.A. *Eighth Edition.*

"In publishing these two little volumes Mr. Saunders has done English readers a genuine service. . . . He has also introduced his translation by a clear and thoroughly helpful preface, in which are defined with sufficient exactness Schopenhauer's philosophic standpoint and the relation of his minor writings to his chief metaphysical treatise. . . . Schopenhauer is commonly ranked among the few philosophers, including our own Berkeley, who possess a literary style. The aphorisms give an excellent sample of this style. By their very form they exhibit at its best Schopenhauer's characteristic manner—his directness, his momentum, his brevity. . . . Even in point of substance, it contains many a keen observation, and enforces unpalatable, but eminently wholesome truths. . . . Nor do we remember to have met with a finer plea, on the whole, for that inner self-culture which is the great and unfailing condition of human happiness."—*Athenæum.*

"It was a happy thought which inspired Mr. Saunders to translate some of Schopenhauer's minor essays. He has succeeded in a remarkable degree in retaining the pungent flavour of the original, and at the same time in dressing his dish for the English palate." —*Academy.*

"Let your view of Schopenhauer be what it may, you cannot help enjoying and admiring the wealth of observation, reflection, and wisdom in 'Counsels and Maxims'."—*Truth.*

RELIGION: a Dialogue, and other Essays.
By ARTHUR SCHOPENHAUER. Selected and Translated by T. BAILEY SAUNDERS, M.A. *Eighth Ed. Enlarged.*

" In this modest volume we have a selection of very readable essays from the writings of the famous pessimistic philosopher, clothed in good, intelligible English."—*Literary World.*

" Mr. Saunders' extracts from Schopenhauer's *Parerga und Paralipomena* make a most readable booklet. They do not deal with the more technical aspects of his philosophy . . . but contain some of Schopenhauer's brilliant *obiter dicta* on matters of more immediate popular interest."—*Scots Observer.*

" There is no doubt either as to the public interest taken in Schopenhauer or as to the services rendered to his memory by Mr. Saunders. This is a very handy and useful little book."—*Spectator.*

" The essays are eminently readable and full of clever things. To the translator we cannot pay a higher compliment than by saying that he never makes us aware of his existence."—*Igdrasil.*

THE ART OF LITERATURE. A Series of Essays. By ARTHUR SCHOPENHAUER. Selected and Translated by T. BAILEY SAUNDERS. *Seventh Edition.*

" Mr. Saunders has fitly brought his Schopenhauer series to a close with a group of essays on literature. The essays on authorship, style, criticism and genius are among the most attractive and suggestive of his writing."—*Athenæum.*

" This final instalment on the art of literature exhibits the sage at his best. Mr. Saunders has evidently regarded his translation as a labour of love, and has done full justice to it."—*Liverpool Post.*

" The translator has done excellent service to the great pessimist's reputation in this country. Whatever else these pages do, they provoke thought, and their bitterness is more often a tonic than an irritant."—*Inquirer.*

STUDIES IN PESSIMISM. A Series of Essays. By Arthur Schopenhauer. Selected and Translated by T. Bailey Saunders. *Tenth Edition.*

"We have once more to thank Mr. Saunders for a series of extracts, mostly from the 'Parerga'. Like the former translations this one is extremely well done, and the volume should be popular."—*Glasgow Herald.*

"If others have been the prophets of Schopenhauer to the mass of English readers, Mr. Saunders may fairly claim to have been the philosopher's interpreter. He has known how to make the pessimist not only intelligible, but attractive to the general reader by administering Schopenhauer's wisdom in small doses, and in a form not too highly concentrated. The series of little books by which Mr. Saunders has done this still goes on. The latest number is by no means the least interesting of them all, and as Mr. Saunders' version is again admirable. He unites readable idiomatic English, untainted by any infection of Teutonism that might easily have weakened the style."—*Scotsman.*

ON HUMAN NATURE. Essays in Ethics and Politics. Selected and Translated by T. Bailey Saunders, M.A. *Sixth Edition.*

"The latest volume of the Schopenhauer Series appears to maintain the standard reached by earlier volumes. Schopenhauer on his lighter side, not as a philosopher, but as a man of the world and moralist, is rapidly becoming popular with English readers, in consequence of the care with which Mr. Saunders administers small doses of the *Parerga und Paralipomena* in the guise of most readable essays. Always pregnant and thought-provoking, they are tonic even when they irritate most."—*Cambridge Review.*

GEORGE ALLEN & UNWIN LTD., LONDON.

The Two Babylons
Alexander Hislop
You may be surprised to learn that many traditions of Roman Catholicism in fact don't come from Christ's teachings but from an ancient Babylonian "Mystery" religion that was centered on Nimrod, his wife Semiramis, and a child Tammuz. This book shows how this ancient religion transformed itself as it incorporated Christ into its teachings...

Religion/History   Pages:358

ISBN: *1-59462-010-5*   MSRP *$22.95*

QTY

The Power Of Concentration
Theron Q. Dumont
It is of the utmost value to learn how to concentrate. To make the greatest success of anything you must be able to concentrate your entire thought upon the idea you are working on. The person that is able to concentrate utilizes all constructive thoughts and shuts out all destructive ones...

Self Help/Inspirational   Pages:196

ISBN: *1-59462-141-1*   MSRP *$14.95*

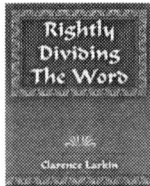

Rightly Dividing The Word
Clarence Larkin
The "Fundamental Doctrines" of the Christian Faith are clearly outlined in numerous books on Theology, but they are not available to the average reader and were mainly written for students. The Author has made it the work of his ministry to preach the "Fundamental Doctrines". To this end he has aimed to express them in the simplest and clearest manner...

Religion   Pages:352

ISBN: *1-59462-334-1*   MSRP *$23.45*

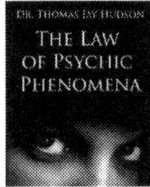

The Law of Psychic Phenomena
Thomson Jay Hudson
"I do not expect this book to stand upon its literary merits; for if it is unsound in principle, felicity of diction cannot save it, and if sound, homeliness of expression cannot destroy it. My primary object in offering it to the public is to assist in bringing Psychology within the domain of the exact sciences. That this has never been accomplished..."

New Age   Pages:420

ISBN: *1-59462-124-1*   MSRP *$29.95*

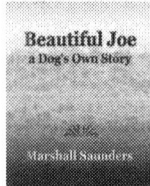

Beautiful Joe
Marshall Saunders
When Marshall visited the Moore family in 1892, she discovered Joe, a dog had nursed back to health from his previous abusive home to live a happy life. So moved was she, that she wrote this classic masterpiece which won accolades and was recognized as a heartwarming symbol for humane animal treatment...

Fiction   Pages:256

ISBN: *1-59462-261-2*   MSRP *$18.45*

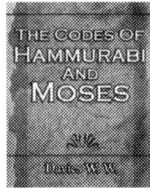

The Codes Of Hammurabi And
Moses - W. W. Davies
The discovery of the Hammurabi Code is one of the greatest achievements of archaeology, and is of paramount interest, not only to the student of the Bible, but also to all those interested in ancient history...

Religion   Pages:132

ISBN: *1-59462-338-4*   MSRP *$12.95*

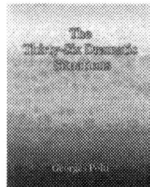

The Thirty-Six Dramatic Situations
Georges Polti
An incredibly useful guide for aspiring authors and playwrights. This volume categorizes every dramatic situation which could occur in a story and describes them in a list of 36 situations. A great aid to help inspire or formalize the creative writing process...

Self Help/Reference   Pages:204

ISBN: *1-59462-134-9*   MSRP *$15.95*

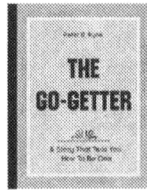

The Go-Getter
Kyne B. Peter
The Go Getter is the story of William Peck. He was a war veteran and amputee who will not be refused what he wants. Peck not only fights to find employment but continually proves himself more than competent at the many difficult test that are throw his way in the course of his early days with the Ricks Lumber Company...

Business/Self Help/Inspirational   Pages:68

ISBN: *1-59462-186-1*   MSRP *$8.95*

QTY

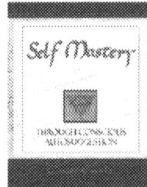

Self Mastery
Emile Coue
Emile Coue came up with novel way to improve the lives of people. He was a pharmacist by trade and often saw ailing people. This lead him to develop autosuggestion, a form of self-hypnosis. At the time his theories weren't popular but over the years evidence is mounting that he was indeed right all along...

New Age/Self Help   Pages:98

ISBN: *1-59462-189-6*   MSRP *$7.95*

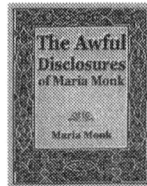

The Awful Disclosures Of
Maria Monk
"I cannot banish the scenes and characters of this book from my memory. To me it can never appear like an amusing fable, or lose its interest and importance. The story is one which is continually before me, and must return fresh to my mind with painful emotions as long as I live.."

Religion   Pages:232

ISBN: *1-59462-160-8*   MSRP *$17.95*

As a Man Thinketh
James Allen
"This little volume (the result of meditation and experience) is not intended as an exhaustive treatise on the much-written-upon subject of the power of thought. It is suggestive rather than explanatory, its object being to stimulate men and women to the discovery and perception of the truth that by virtue of the thoughts which they choose and encourage..."

Inspirational/Self Help   Pages:80

ISBN: *1-59462-231-0*   MSRP *$9.45*

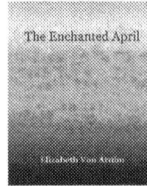

The Enchanted April
Elizabeth Von Arnim
It began in a woman's club in London on a February afternoon, an uncomfortable club, and a miserable afternoon when Mrs. Wilkins, who had come down from Hampstead to shop and had lunched at her club, took up The Times from the table in the smoking-room...

Fiction   Pages:368

ISBN: *1-59462-150-0*   MSRP *$23.45*

Holland - The History Of Netherlands
Thomas Colley Grattan
Thomas Grattan was a prestigious writer from Dublin who served as British Consul to the US. Among his works is an authoritative look at the history of Holland. A colorful and interesting look at history...

History/Politics   Pages:408

ISBN: *1-59462-137-3*   MSRP *$26.95*

A Concise Dictionary of Middle English
A. L. Mayhew
Walter W. Skeat
The present work is intended to meet, in some measure, the requirements of those who wish to make some study of Middle-English, and who find a difficulty in obtaining such assistance as will enable them to find out the meanings and etymologies of the words most essential to their purpose...

Reference/History   Pages:332

ISBN: *1-59462-119-5*   MSRP *$29.95*

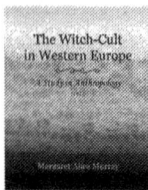

The Witch-Cult in Western Europe
Margaret Murray

The mass of existing material on this subject is so great that I have not attempted to make a survey of the whole of European "Witchcraft" but have confined myself to an intensive study of the cult in Great Britain. In order, however, to obtain a clearer understanding of the ritual and beliefs I have had recourse to French and Flemish sources...

Occult   Pages:308

ISBN: *1-59462-126-8*   MSRP *$22.45*

QTY

Philosophy Of Natural Therapeutics
Henry Lindlahr

We invite the earnest cooperation in this great work of all those who have awakened to the necessity for more rational living and for radical reform in healing methods...

Health/Philosophy/Self Help   Pages:552

ISBN: *1-59462-132-2*   MSRP *$34.95*

QTY

The Science Of Psychic Healing
Yogi Ramacharaka

This book is not a book of theories it deals with facts. Its author regards the best of theories as but working hypotheses to be used only until better ones present themselves. The "fact" is the principal thing, the essential thing to uncover which the tool, theory, is used...

New Age/Health   Pages:180

ISBN: *1-59462-140-3*   MSRP *$13.95*

A Message to Garcia
Elbert Hubbard

This literary trifle, A Message to Garcia, was written one evening after supper, in a single hour. It was on the Twenty-second of February, Eighteen Hundred Ninety-nine, Washington's Birthday, and we were just going to press with the March Philistine...

New Age/Fiction   Pages:92

ISBN: *1-59462-144-6*   MSRP *$9.95*

Bible Myths
Thomas Doane

In pursuing the study of the Bible Myths, facts pertaining thereto, in a condensed form, seemed to be greatly needed, and nowhere to be found. Widely scattered through hundreds of ancient and modern volumes, most of the contents of this book may indeed be found; but any previous attempt to trace exclusively the myths and legends...

Religion/History   Pages:644

ISBN: *1-59462-163-2*   MSRP *$38.95*

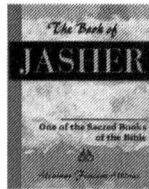

The Book of Jasher
Alcuinus Flaccus Albinus

The Book of Jasher is an historical religious volume that many consider as a missing holy book from the Old Testament. Particularly studied by the Church of Later Day Saints and historians, it covers the history of the world from creation until the period of Judges in Israel. It's authenticity is bolstered due to a reference to the Book of Jasher in the Bible in Joshua 10:13

Religion/History   Pages:276

ISBN: *1-59462-197-7*   MSRP *$18.95*

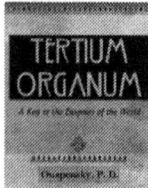

Tertium Organum
P. D. Ouspensky

A truly mind expanding writing that combines science with mysticism with unprecedented elegance. He presents the world we live in as a multi dimensional world and time as a motion through this world. But this isn't a cold and purely analytical explanation but a masterful presentation filled with similies and analogies...

New Age   Pages:356

ISBN: *1-59462-205-1*   MSRP *$23.95*

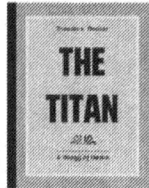

The Titan
Theodore Dreiser

"When Frank Algernon Cowperwood emerged from the Eastern District Penitentiary, in Philadelphia he realized that the old life he had lived in that city since boyhood was ended. His youth was gone, and with it had been lost the great business prospects of his earlier manhood. He must begin again..."

Fiction   Pages:564

ISBN: *1-59462-220-5*   MSRP *$33.95*

Advance Course in Yogi Philosophy
Yogi Ramacharaka

"The twelve lessons forming this volume were originally issued in the shape of monthly lessons, known as "The Advanced Course in Yogi Philosophy and Oriental Occultism" during a period of twelve months beginning with October, 1904, and ending September, 1905."

Philosophy/Inspirational/Self Help   Pages:340

ISBN: *1-59462-229-9*   MSRP *$22.95*

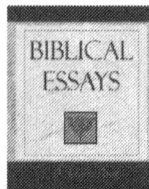

Biblical Essays
J. B. Lightfoot

About one-third of the present volume has already seen the light. The opening essay "On the Internal Evidence for the Authenticity and Genuineness of St John's Gospel" was published in the "Expositor" in the early months of 1890, and has been reprinted since...

Religion/History   Pages:480

ISBN: *1-59462-238-8*   MSRP *$30.95*

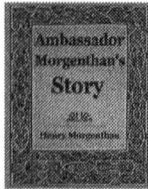

Ambassador Morgenthau's Story
Henry Morgenthau

"By this time the American people have probably become convinced that the Germans deliberately planned the conquest of the world. Yet they hesitate to convict on circumstantial evidence and for this reason all eye witnesses to this, the greatest crime in modern history, should volunteer their testimony..."

History   Pages:472

ISBN: *1-59462-244-2*   MSRP *$29.95*

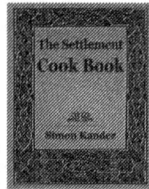

The Settlement Cook Book
Simon Kander

A legacy from the civil war, this book is a classic "American charity cookbook," which was used for fundraisers starting in Milwaukee. While it has transformed over the years, this printing provides great recipes from American history. Over two million copies have been sold. This volume contains a rich collection of recipes from noted chefs and hostesses of the turn of the century...

How-to   Pages:472

ISBN: *1-59462-256-6*   MSRP *$29.95*

The Aquarian Gospel of Jesus the Christ
Levi Dowling

A retelling of Jesus' story which tells us what happened during the twenty year gap left by the Bible's New Testament. It tells of his travels to the far-east where he studied with the masters and fought against the rigid caste system. This book has enjoyed a resurgence in modern America and provides spiritual insight with charm. Its influences can be seen throughout the Age of Aquarius.

Religion   Pages:264

ISBN: *1-59462-321-X*   MSRP *$18.95*

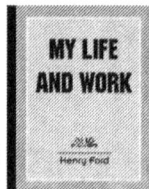

My Life and Work
Henry Ford

Henry Ford revolutionized the world with his implementation of mass production for the Model T automobile. Gain valuable business insight into his life and work with his own auto-biography... We have only started on our development of our country we have not as yet, with all our talk of wonderful progress, done more than scratch the surface. The progress has been wonderful enough but..."

Biographies/History/Business   Pages:300

ISBN: *1-59462-198-5*   MSRP *$21.95*

QTY

The Rosicrucian Cosmo-Conception Mystic Christianity *by Max Heindel*
ISBN: *1-59462-188-8* **$38.95**
The Rosicrucian Cosmo-conception is not dogmatic, neither does it appeal to any other authority than the reason of the student. It is: not controversial, but is: sent forth in the, hope that it may help to clear..
New Age/Religion Pages 646

Abandonment To Divine Providence *by Jean-Pierre de Caussade*
ISBN: *1-59462-228-0* **$25.95**
"The Rev. Jean Pierre de Caussade was one of the most remarkable spiritual writers of the Society of Jesus in France in the 18th Century. His death took place at Toulouse in 1751. His works have gone through many editions and have been republished...
Inspirational/Religion Pages 400

Mental Chemistry *by Charles Haanel*
ISBN: *1-59462-192-6* **$23.95**
Mental Chemistry allows the change of material conditions by combining and appropriately utilizing the power of the mind. Much like applied chemistry creates something new and unique out of careful combinations of chemicals the mastery of mental chemistry..
New Age Pages 354

The Letters of Robert Browning and Elizabeth Barret Barrett 1845-1846 vol II
ISBN: *1-59462-193-4* **$35.95**
by Robert Browning and Elizabeth Barrett
Biographies Pages 596

Gleanings In Genesis (volume I) *by Arthur W. Pink*
ISBN: *1-59462-130-6* **$27.45**
Appropriately has Genesis been termed "the seed plot of the Bible" for in it we have, in germ form, almost all of the great doctrines which are afterwards fully developed in the books of Scripture which follow..
Religion/Inspirational Pages 420

The Master Key *by L. W. de Laurence*
ISBN: *1-59462-001-6* **$30.95**
In no branch of human knowledge has there been a more lively increase of the spirit of research during the past few years than in the study of Psychology. Concentration and Mental Discipline. The requests for authentic lessons in Thought Control, Mental Discipline and...
New Age/Business Pages 422

The Lesser Key Of Solomon Goetia *by L. W. de Laurence*
ISBN: *1-59462-092-X* **$9.95**
This translation of the first book of the "Lernegton" which is now for the first time made accessible to students of Talismanic Magic was done, after careful collation and edition, from numerous Ancient Manuscripts in Hebrew, Latin, and French...
New Age/Occult Pages 92

Rubaiyat Of Omar Khayyam *by Edward Fitzgerald*
ISBN: *1-59462-332-5* **$13.95**
Edward Fitzgerald, whom the world has already learned, in spite of his own efforts to remain within the shadow of anonymity, to look upon as one of the rarest poets of the century, was born at Bredfield, in Suffolk, on the 31st of March, 1809. He was the third son of John Purcell...
Music Pages 172

Ancient Law *by Henry Maine*
ISBN: *1-59462-128-4* **$29.95**
The chief object of the following pages is to indicate some of the earliest ideas of mankind, as they are reflected in Ancient Law, and to point out the relation of those ideas to modern thought.
Religion/History Pages 452

Far-Away Stories *by William J. Locke*
ISBN: *1-59462-129-2* **$19.45**
"Good wine needs no bush, but a collection of mixed vintages does. And this book is just such a collection. Some of the stories I do not want to remain buried for ever in the museum files of dead magazine-numbers an author's not unpardonable vanity..."
Fiction Pages 272

Life of David Crockett *by David Crockett*
ISBN: *1-59462-250-7* **$27.45**
"Colonel David Crockett was one of the most remarkable men of the times in which he lived. Born in humble life, but gifted with a strong will, an indomitable courage, and unremitting perseverance...
Biographies/New Age Pages 424

Lip-Reading *by Edward Nitchie*
ISBN: *1-59462-206-X* **$25.95**
Edward B. Nitchie, founder of the New York School for the Hard of Hearing, now the Nitchie School of Lip-Reading, Inc, wrote "LIP-READING Principles and Practice". The development and perfecting of this meritorious work on lip-reading was an undertaking...
How-to Pages 400

A Handbook of Suggestive Therapeutics, Applied Hypnotism, Psychic Science
ISBN: *1-59462-214-0* **$24.95**
by Henry Munro
Health/New Age/Health/Self-help Pages 376

A Doll's House: and Two Other Plays *by Henrik Ibsen*
ISBN: *1-59462-112-8* **$19.95**
Henrik Ibsen created this classic when in revolutionary 1848 Rome. Introducing some striking concepts in playwriting for the realist genre, this play has been studied the world over.
Fiction/Classics/Plays 308

The Light of Asia *by sir Edwin Arnold*
ISBN: *1-59462-204-3* **$13.95**
In this poetic masterpiece, Edwin Arnold describes the life and teachings of Buddha. The man who was to become known as Buddha to the world was born as Prince Gautama of India but he rejected the worldly riches and abandoned the reigns of power when...
Religion/History/Biographies Pages 170

The Complete Works of Guy de Maupassant *by Guy de Maupassant*
ISBN: *1-59462-157-8* **$16.95**
"For days and days, nights and nights, I had dreamed of that first kiss which was to consecrate our engagement, and I knew not on what spot I should put my lips..."
Fiction/Classics Pages 240

The Art of Cross-Examination *by Francis L. Wellman*
ISBN: *1-59462-309-0* **$26.95**
Written by a renowned trial lawyer, Wellman imparts his experience and uses case studies to explain how to use psychology to extract desired information through questioning.
How-to/Science/Reference Pages 408

Answered or Unanswered? *by Louisa Vaughan*
ISBN: *1-59462-248-5* **$10.95**
Miracles of Faith in China
Religion Pages 112

The Edinburgh Lectures on Mental Science (1909) *by Thomas*
ISBN: *1-59462-008-3* **$11.95**
This book contains the substance of a course of lectures recently given by the writer in the Queen Street Hall, Edinburgh. Its purpose is to indicate the Natural Principles governing the relation between Mental Action and Material Conditions...
New Age/Psychology Pages 148

Ayesha *by H. Rider Haggard*
ISBN: *1-59462-301-5* **$24.95**
Verily and indeed it is the unexpected that happens! Probably if there was one person upon the earth from whom the Editor of this, and of a certain previous history, did not expect to hear again...
Classics Pages 380

Ayala's Angel *by Anthony Trollope*
ISBN: *1-59462-352-X* **$29.95**
The two girls were both pretty, but Lucy who was twenty-one who supposed to be simple and comparatively unattractive, whereas Ayala was credited, as her Bombwhat romantic name might show, with poetic charm and a taste for romance. Ayala when her father died was nineteen...
Fiction Pages 484

The American Commonwealth *by James Bryce*
ISBN: *1-59462-286-8* **$34.45**
An interpretation of American democratic political theory. It examines political mechanics and society from the perspective of Scotsman James Bryce
Politics Pages 572

Stories of the Pilgrims *by Margaret P. Pumphrey*
ISBN: *1-59462-116-0* **$17.95**
This book explores pilgrims religious oppression in England as well as their escape to Holland and eventual crossing to America on the Mayflower, and their early days in New England...
History Pages 268

Bringing Classics to Life

BOOK JUNGLE

www.bookjungle.com *email: sales@bookjungle.com fax: 630-214-0564 mail: Book Jungle PO Box 2226 Champaign, IL 61825*

QTY

The Fasting Cure *by Sinclair Upton*   ISBN: *1-59462-222-1* **$13.95**
In the Cosmopolitan Magazine for May, 1910, and in the Contemporary Review (London) for April, 1910, I published an article dealing with my experiences in fasting, I have written a great many magazine articles, but never one which attracted so much attention... New Age/Self Help/Health Pages 164

Hebrew Astrology *by Sepharial*   ISBN: *1-59462-308-2* **$13.45**
In these days of advanced thinking it is a matter of common observation that we have left many of the old landmarks behind and that we are now pressing forward to greater heights and to a wider horizon than that which represented the mind-content of our progenitors... Astrology Pages 144

Thought Vibration or The Law of Attraction in the Thought World   ISBN: *1-59462-127-6* **$12.95**
by William Walker Atkinson   Psychology/Religion Pages 144

Optimism *by Helen Keller*   ISBN: *1-59462-108-X* **$15.95**
Helen Keller was blind, deaf, and mute since 19 months old, yet famously learned how to overcome these handicaps, communicate with the world, and spread her lectures promoting optimism. An inspiring read for everyone... Biographies/Inspirational Pages 84

Sara Crewe *by Frances Burnett*   ISBN: *1-59462-360-0* **$9.45**
In the first place, Miss Minchin lived in London. Her home was a large, dull, tall one, in a large, dull square, where all the houses were alike, and all the sparrows were alike, and where all the door-knockers made the same heavy sound... Childrens/Classic Pages 86

The Autobiography of Benjamin Franklin *by Benjamin Franklin*   ISBN: *1-59462-135-7* **$24.95**
The Autobiography of Benjamin Franklin has probably been more extensively read than any other American historical work, and no other book of its kind has had such ups and downs of fortune. Franklin lived for many years in England, where he was agent... Biographies/History Pages 332

Name	
Email	
Telephone	
Address	
City, State ZIP	

☐ **Credit Card**   ☐ **Check / Money Order**

Credit Card Number	
Expiration Date	
Signature	

Please Mail to: Book Jungle
PO Box 2226
Champaign, IL 61825
or Fax to: 630-214-0564

ORDERING INFORMATION

web: *www.bookjungle.com*
email: *sales@bookjungle.com*
fax: *630-214-0564*
mail: *Book Jungle PO Box 2226 Champaign, IL 61825*
or PayPal *to sales@bookjungle.com*

Please contact us for bulk discounts

DIRECT-ORDER TERMS

**20% Discount if You Order
Two or More Books**
Free Domestic Shipping!
Accepted: Master Card, Visa,
Discover, American Express

www.ingramcontent.com/pod-product-compliance
Lightning Source LLC
LaVergne TN
LVHW061225060426
835509LV00012B/1423